Men Are Like Waffles Women Are Like Spaghetti

Understanding and Delighting in Your Differences

Bill and Pam Farrel

Love_Wise Resources®
Oxnard, CA

Published by Love-Wise®
© 2007 • Bill and Pam Farrel
Reprinted 2014, 2016

ISBN 978-1-5370-0620-8

Dewey Decimal Classification: 306.81
Subject Headings: MEN \ WOMEN \ MARRIAGE

Unless otherwise noted, all Scripture quotations are taken from the
Holman Christian Standard Bible®, copyright © 1999, 2000, 2001, 2002, 2003
by Holman Bible Publishers. Used by permission.

Scripture quotations identified NIV are taken from
The New International Version © International Bible
Publishers 1973, 1978, 1984. Used by permission.

Scripture quotations identified NKJV are taken from the
New King James Version. Copyright © 1979, 1980, 1982,
Thomas Nelson, Inc., Publishers.

To order additional copies of this resource:
visit www.love-wise.com/wsbook.php

Printed in the United States of America

Love_Wise Resources
3600 Harbor Blvd. #116
Oxnard, CA 93035

Contents

LEADER GUIDE

About the Authors

PAM AND BILL FARREL are international speakers, relationship specialists, and best-selling authors of over 40 books including *Men Are Like Waffles–Women Are Like Spaghetti*; *Red-Hot Monogamy*; *The 10 Best Decisoins a Couple Can Make*; *Single Men Are Like Waffles–Single Women Are Like Spaghetti*; *The Secret Language of Successful Couples*; *Simple Skills for Every Man/Woman*; and *The 10 Best Decisions a Parent Can Make*.

The Farrels have a regular newspaper column on relationships appearing in several cities. Their writing has been published in numerous magazines. They are also regularly featured on radio and TV. Audiences are delighted by the Farrels' combination of personal warmth, sense of humor, practical illustrations, and relevant biblical application. Their style and insights span age, cultural, and denominational boundaries. Audiences of all shapes and sizes are impacted and encouraged by their message.

Bill has served as a senior pastor, youth pastor, and small groups pastor, and Pam has been a director of women's ministries as well as a sought after speaker for women's events. The Farrels have been working with couples and families for over 27 years. Bill and Pam are also the cofounders and codirectors of Love-Wise, an organization that helps build successful relationships.

Bill and Pam have been married for more than 3 decades and have helped countless couples discvoer the simple skills that make real realtionships work. To relax, Pam and Bill love to kayak , ride bikes and take long walks at the beach together. They would love to hear from you at love-wise.com

AMY SUMMERS worked with the Farrels to write the learning activities and leader guide for this study. Although Amy's primary career is chauffeur and social secretary for her children Aaron, Rachel, and Philip, she is also an experienced writer and Sunday School leader. In addition to her parenting and writing responsibilities, Amy works part-time as a writing tutor at the local elementary school. Amy is a graduate of Baylor University and Southwestern Baptist Theological Seminary. She and her husband, Stephen, raise their children in Arden, North Carolina.

About the Study

Welcome to Men Are Like Waffles–Women Are Like Spaghetti! Before you begin your study, there are a couple of things we would like to point out. First of all, this study is designed for five days of individual study and one small-group session per week. However, the six weeks of individual study are not divided into daily segments. You will benefit most from the material if you study a portion each day rather than trying to complete all the material at one sitting. This will give you more time to concentrate on the message and listen for what the Lord has to say to you. The personal learning activities are designed to help you apply to your life what you are learning. Please don't skip over these activities. They will also help prepare you for your small-group sessions. Most of the activities will be the same for you and your spouse, but there are a few throughout the study that will be specifically targeted for the husband and others for the wife. In some instances you will be asked to compare answers with your spouse. Please take the time to complete this step. That time together will be an invaluable opportunity for communicating with your spouse about crucial issues in your relationship.

Consider the following suggestions to make your study more meaningful:

• Trust the Holy Spirit to be your teacher. Ask Him for guidance as you seek to learn how to better relate to your spouse. Release your mind and heart in ready obedience to all He will teach you.
• Pray sincerely both alone and with your spouse. Base your prayers on what the Holy Spirit is revealing to you through your study.
• Keep a spiritual journal of God's activity in your life as well as your response to Him throughout the study. When God speaks, it is important to record it. Your memory will not always recall these special moments, but your journal will.
• Live out your growing relationship with and knowledge of God. Share freely with your spouse what the Lord is teaching you. Be willing to step out of your comfort zone as you learn how to best express your love. Expect God to honor your faithful obedience to Him.

It is our hope and prayer that you will laugh and cry (but mostly laugh) as you take the journey with us down the road toward better understanding why men are like waffles and women are like spaghetti. We pray as you learn more about what makes your spouse tick that you will grow to love and appreciate him or her even more. May God bless you as you seek to make your relatoinship all God intends it to be.

week one
Appreciating the Differences

Accept one another, just as the Messiah
also accepted you, to the glory of God.

Romans 15:7

Viewer Guide

God created man in His own image;
He created him in the image of God;
He created them male and female.
Genesis 1:27

Husbands, when it's your wife's turn to talk:
pack your bags and go on a listening journey.

Wives, when it's your husband's turn to talk:
stay in the box!

The key to communication is to take turns listening.

Four Levels of Communication:

1. _____

2. _____

3. _____

4. _____

Four Steps to Being a Great Listener:

1. _____

2. _____

3. _____

4. _____

At the beginning of history God said, "Let Us make man in Our image, according to Our likeness … So God created man in His own image; He created him in the image of God; He created them male and female" (Gen. 1:26-27). It was in God's plan to make men and women different from the moment He imagined us. The original plan was to use these differences as a starting point for building intimate, fulfilling relationships. Unfortunately, what started out as an advantage has turned out to be a universal source of frustration.

Despite the frustration, the vast majority of us have an undeniable desire to have great relationships with the opposite sex. We want both male and female friends; we want successful business relationships with both men and women; and we want marriages that are happy and harmonious. That is why so many of our decisions are affected by how the opposite sex will respond.

It is possible to make too much out of the differences between men and women, but it is also possible to make the opposite mistake. If you want to have relationships that add to your life rather than make you exhausted, the place to start is with an understanding of the uniqueness each gender brings to the relationship.

Read Romans 15:7 at the top of page 6.

What is the goal of discovering the unique differences of

your spouse? _____

How did Christ accept you? _____

What will happen when you and your spouse choose to accept one another—differences, weaknesses, warts, and all?

_____

_____

Pause now and pray, asking God to use this study to help you accept your spouse with the same generous, accepting spirit with which Jesus accepts you. Pray that God will be glorified by how you and your spouse accept and celebrate one another's differences.

Dive into the Differences

So, how are you to grasp the differences between men and women? We like to think of them this way: men are like waffles, women are like spaghetti. At first this may seem silly, even juvenile, but stay with us. It is a picture that works and men get it (because it involves food).

MEN ARE LIKE WAFFLES

Men process life in boxes. If you look down at a waffle, you see a collection of boxes separated by walls. The boxes are separate from each other and make convenient holding places. That is typically how men process life. Their thinking is divided up into boxes that have room for one issue and one issue only. The first issue of life goes in the first box, the second goes in the second box, and so on.

The typical man lives in one box at a time and one box only. When a man is at work, he is at work. When he is in the garage tinkering, he is in the garage tinkering. When he is watching TV, he is simply watching TV. That is why he looks as though he is in a trance and can ignore everything else going on around him. Social scientists call this compartmentalizing—that is, putting life and responsibilities into different compartments.

A man will strategically organize his life in boxes and then spend most of his time in the boxes in which he can succeed. Success is such a strong motivation for him that he will seek out boxes that work and ignore boxes that confuse him or make him feel like a failure.

The drive to succeed is why men find it so easy to develop hobbies that consume their time. If a man finds something he is good at, it makes him feel good about himself and about his life. Because men tend to be good with mechanical and spatial activities, they get emotionally attached to building, fixing, and chasing things. Yard projects become expressions of their personalities. Their car becomes their signature.

The bottom line is this: men feel best about themselves when they are solving problems. Therefore, they spend most of their time doing what they are best at while they attempt to ignore the things that cause them to feel deficient.

WOMEN ARE LIKE SPAGHETTI

Women process life more like a plate of pasta. If you look at a plate of spaghetti, you notice there are lots of individual noodles that all touch one another. If you attempt to follow one noodle around the plate, you will intersect a lot of other noodles, and you might even switch to another noodle seamlessly. Women face life in this way. Every thought and issue is connected to every other thought and issue in some way. Life is much more of a process for women than it is for men.

This is why a woman is typically better at multitasking than a man. She can talk on the phone, prepare a meal, make a shopping list, work on the agenda for tomorrow's business meeting, give instructions to her children as they are going out to play, and close the door with her foot without skipping a beat. As a result, most women are in pursuit of connecting life together. They solve problems from a much different perspective than men.

Women consistently sense the need to talk things through. In conversation they can link together the logical, emotional, relational, and spiritual aspects of the issue. The links come naturally, so the conversation is effortless. If they are able to connect all the issues, the answer to the question at hand bubbles to the surface and is readily accepted.

This often creates significant stress for couples. While she is making all the connections, he is frantically jumping boxes trying to keep up with the conversation. The man's eyes are rolling back in his head while a tidal wave of information is swallowing him up. When she is done, she feels better and he is overwhelmed. The conversation might look something like this:

"Honey, the other day I was driving by your favorite truck store—the one where you got that cool cup holder that goes on the window; and that truck store is right next to my favorite dress shop. You know, the one with the cute two-piece suit in the window? That suit is my color. You know, last week I went to that seminar on colors to find out what colors look good on me and what colors don't, and they said I was a 'summer' and that suit is a summer color so I knew if I bought it and put it on you'd say, 'Oh baby, you look so fine!' and I love it when you say that. I was thinking that suit looks a lot like the one Mrs. Clinton wore when she was saying she communicated with Eleanor Roosevelt for inspiration. I don't know, that seems kind of weird because Eleanor is dead. Isn't that kind of like some of that New Age stuff we heard about in church on Sunday? That kind of stuff is creeping into the schools. Maybe we should stop and pray for the kids!"

The whole time his wife is praying, he's thinking, "So what about my truck?"

One thing that creates havoc in male/female interaction is the fact that most men have boxes in their waffle that have no words. These boxes contain thoughts about the past, their work, and pleasant experiences, but these thoughts do not turn into words.

Not all of the wordless boxes have thoughts, however. There are actually boxes in the average man's waffle that contain no words and no thoughts. These boxes are just as blank as a white sheet of paper. They are EMPTY! To help relieve stress in his life, a man will park in these boxes to relax. Amazingly, his wife always seems to notice when he is in park. She observes his blank look and the relaxed posture he has taken on the couch. She assumes this is a good time to talk as he is so relaxed, and so she invariably asks, "What are you thinking, sweetheart?"

He immediately panics because he knows if he tells the truth she will think he is lying. She cannot imagine a moment without words in her mind. If he says, "nothing," she thinks he is hiding something and is afraid to talk about it. She becomes instantly curious and mildly suspicious. Not wanting to disappoint his wife, his eyes start darting back and forth hoping to find a box in close proximity that has words in it. If he finds a box of words quickly, he will engage his wife in conversation and both will feel good about the relationship. If he is slow in finding words, her suspicion fails to be extinguished and he feels a sense of failure. He desperately wants to explain to his wife that he sometimes just goes blank. Nothing is wrong, he isn't in denial, and nothing is being hidden. This is the way he has been his whole life, but she cannot imagine it.

These blank boxes have an interesting characteristic that often gets in the way of meaningful conversation. In the middle of conversation a man will periodically be moving from one box to another, and in between two boxes of words he passes through one of these blank boxes. Right in the middle of conversation, he goes silent. He knows he should have something to say, but he is blank.

DIFFERENT BY DESIGN

The differences between men and women are not limited to conversation. Men and women think differently, process emotions differently, make decisions differently, and learn differently. Yet men and women complement one another so beautifully that a healthy relationship makes both partners more complete.

The differences start in the physical structure of the brain. "Research is confirming that the brains of men and women are subtly different … For example, studies show that human male brains are, on average, approximately ten percent larger than female brains. Certain brain areas in women, however, contain more nerve cells."[1]

The differences then extend to the operation of the brain. "One study shows that men and women perform equally well in a test that asks subjects to read a list of nonsense words and determine if they rhyme. Yet, imaging results found that women use areas on the right and left sides of the brain, while men only use areas on the left side to complete the test."[2] Even when it comes to the use of the brain, women connect both sides while men keep it as simple as possible by using only one side.

It then follows that men and women excel at different tasks. "Tests show that women generally can recall lists of words or paragraphs of text better than men. On the other hand, men usually perform better on tests that require the ability to mentally rotate an image in order to solve a problem."[3] Consequently, men use different strategies and different parts of their brains to navigate, and they really are better at finding their way when they are lost. Men use geometry to figure it out, such as following a map, while women depend on their memory advantage and landmarks. And it appears this difference is associated with the different parts of the brains that are used.[4]

As you work through this study, you will be exposed to the most important differences between you and your spouse. We hope you will laugh with us, because developing a good sense of humor is one of the best ways to break the tension that exists in the battle of the sexes. We hope you will gain insight into your mate and develop skills that will make you glad men are like waffles and women are like spaghetti. And most vital of all, we hope you will be thankful to God, our Creator, who formed the differences for our good from the beginning.

Read Genesis 1:27 below. Underline the phrase that expresses the dignity of each gender with all its differences.

God created man in His own image;
He created him in the image of God;
He created them male and female (Gen. 1:27).

How do you most often regard your spouse's differences?
☒ a beautiful illustration of the image of God   ☒ annoying

Write one way your spouse is different from you, and describe why that difference is beneficial to your marriage and family.

_____

_____

Thank God for this difference. Then let your spouse read what you wrote!

Communication

*"If I say something that can be interpreted in two ways,
and one of the ways makes you sad or angry, I meant the other way."
—sign hanging in a local tourist shop*

Men and women have very different approaches to communication. When a man starts a conversation, it is generally because he perceives there is a problem that needs to be addressed. If there is no perceived problem, he feels no particular need to talk. The box he is currently in is at ease, and the lack of distress makes him assume that everything is all right with the relationship. His wife, on the other hand, has a constant desire to talk with her husband. She wants to connect him to everything in her life and assumes he wants to connect her to everything in his life. When she begins a conversation, he assumes she is bringing up a problem that needs to be resolved. Generally, she is starting the conversation because it seems natural to talk about whatever is on her mind. While she is in conversational mode, he turns on the fix-it mechanism and the conflict begins. She gets her feelings hurt because he is trying to figure her out rather than just visit with her. He gets impatient because there seems to be no point. What started out as a hopeful moment for drawing closer becomes another nagging defeat.

PACK YOUR BAGS!

Let me (Bill) talk with the men first. When your wife begins a conversation with you, assume that she needs to connect the issues of her life. She doesn't need you to work your male logic into her thinking process. She simply needs you to help her make the connections. You will do well if you view the conversation as a journey she is going to lead you on. Pack your bags, go on the journey, and encourage her to take the conversation wherever she wants.

Your wife is driven to connect. Because she is aware of all the issues of her life, and because it is impossible to fix every issue in her life all at once, she approaches things differently than you. Before she looks for solutions, she interacts with each part of her life and experiences the appropriate emotion of each issue.

That is why she can experience such a range of emotions in one conversation. Just because you can't keep up with her does not mean your way is better. If you are willing to serve this need, you will be married to a much happier woman.

Men, to help you understand your wife's need to finish conversations, imagine if everything in your life ended early. What if you were never able to finish a meal because it was taken away from you when you were halfway through? What if every sporting event you watched on TV was turned off five minutes before the end of the game? What if every sexual encounter ended before its climax? What if every project you started had to be abandoned before you were able to finish it? Can you sense the frustration and irritation this would bring? If life were actually like this, your anger would always be close to the surface and your motivation to keep pursuing these activities would be shattered. This is how your wife feels when she is not able to finish conversations with you.

So pack your bags, go on a listening journey, and let her take the conversation anyplace she wants it to go! What she is doing is connecting her life to you. You don't have to fix anything—just listen. When you truly listen to your wife, an amazing thing happens. Suddenly you become better looking, wiser, more capable, and sexier in her eyes! There is a big positive payoff for the husband who becomes a good listener!

Circle the statement that best reflects your marriage relationship.

• The husband in this marriage makes the full conversational journey with his wife.

• The husband in this marriage leaves his wife stranded halfway through the journey.

Compare your response with your spouse's. What did you learn about communication in your marriage by comparing your responses?

_____

_____

STAY IN THE BOX

Ladies, when it is your husband's turn to talk, practice staying in the box he wants to open. When he brings up an issue for discussion, he actually intends to talk about that issue. A problem develops because you immediately recognize all the issues related to the one he brought up. You feel the need to open all those boxes because they are relevant to the discussion. Don't do it!

We women are very impatient listeners. We often think that because men don't process life the way we do they are unfeeling and uncaring, but nothing could be farther from the truth. The fact is, we never let them stay in one box long enough to discover their feelings.

If we stay focused on one topic and resist the urge to open up all the surrounding boxes, we buy our men the emotional time they need to work their way through the layers of the box. They then trust us enough to open up the well of emotions that are deep in that box. It's a lot like drilling for oil. When you drill deep enough, you can reach a valuable gusher!

When your husband started the conversation, there was one problem on the table to be solved. When you opened the second box, there were two problems. When you opened the third box, there were three, and so on. Every man has his limit of how many problems he can deal with at once. At some point he crosses the line of how many issues he can handle, and he gets overwhelmed. A man's reaction to being overwhelmed can be varied, but it seems to fall into two categories. He either shuts down or gets angry.

Circle the statement that best reflects your marriage relationship.

• The wife in this marriage stays in the one box her husband opens.

• The wife in this marriage impatiently opens a multitude of boxes.

Compare your response with your spouse's. What did you learn about communication in your marriage by comparing your responses?

_____

_____

ACCEPT IT—DON'T CHANGE IT!

Instead of taking turns listening to each other, most couples spend their time trying to change each other. As his wife is breaking down the walls that allow him to separate the issues in his life, he is trying to cut her spaghetti into squares. They are sincerely trying to make sense of their spouse, but they end up confusing each other more. It is as if she is putting marinara sauce on the waffles, and he is putting syrup on the spaghetti.

Taking turns may be hard work, but not taking turns is agonizing. The couple who wants to find a way to make their differences work for them in communication must become good listeners. The amazing thing is that the same listening techniques work for both sides. For the man who wants to be able to travel in conversation with his wife, he must be a focused listener. For the wife who wants to be able to camp in the same box her husband is in, she must be a focused listener. Let's talk for a minute about what listening is not.

Listening is not an attempt to understand the opposite sex. We have been told numerous times that true intimacy is attained when a couple understands one another. The problem is a man will never fully understand a woman, and a woman will never fully understand a man. Many partners are disappointed with each other because they believed that love meant understanding and they failed to achieve it. When the revelation they were promised is missing, they conclude they weren't meant for each other or they don't have what it takes.

Listening is not an attempt to fix your partner. Avoid asking, "Why do you feel this way?" Our emotions have never had the ability to think. We feel what we feel because of past influences and developmental progress. Emotions are not rational in their makeup—they don't think before they express themselves. The goal in intimate conversation with your spouse is not to analyze emotions and come up with some kind of solution that ensures he or she will never feel this way again. The goal is to grow closer and reaffirm your love.

> The goal in intimate conversation with your spouse
> is to grow closer and reaffirm your love.

Listening is not a personality trait. Listening is a skill. You must practice and, over time, develop your own style. The basic elements of listening are shared by all good listeners, but no two people listen exactly the same way. Your ability to listen strategically is determined by how much value you place on it and how hard you are willing to work at it.

Read the verses from Proverbs below.

"Whoever shows contempt for his neighbor lacks sense, but a man with understanding keeps silent" (Prov. 11:12).

"The one who guards his mouth protects his life; the one who opens his lips invites his own ruin" (Prov. 13:3).

"The one who guards his mouth and tongue keeps himself out of trouble" (Prov. 21:23).

Based on these verses, what would you say is a basic element

of listening? _____

How can guarding your mouth guard your marriage?

_____

Read the following Scripture out loud as a prayer.

"Lᴏʀᴅ, set up a guard for my mouth; keep watch at the door
of my lips" (Ps. 141:3).

LEVELS OF COMMUNICATION

Now let's define what listening is. To develop the kind of listening that builds healthy marriages, we must first understand that communication takes place on four levels.

The first level is small talk. This is where you deal with the straightforward stuff of life. "How is the weather?" "What do we need from the store?" "Who is picking up the kids and taking them to practice?" It is important that small talk remain relatively uncomplicated. Issues like the weather and groceries need to be handled as simply and non-emotionally as possible.

The second level is thoughts and opinions. These areas require a little more than the obvious, but they are not inherently emotional. Questions like, "Where would you like to go to dinner tonight?" "What is your favorite color?" "Which outfit do you like better?" should not throw a couple into a tailspin. We should provide freedom to one another to have our own opinions on these issues without loading them up with emotional freight.

The third level is where people share their opinions and convictions. This is where spiritual and moral convictions are revealed to one another. This is the level at which compatibility is vital for married couples. It is impossible to establish compatibility in all areas of life. Your gender differences, personality differences, family backgrounds, and personal preferences guarantee that some parts of your relationship will be incompatible, but you don't need to see eye-to-eye in every area. You do, however, need significant agreement on the core issues of life. If you differ on your preference for hobbies or your favorite colors or the level to which you like to have your house organized, you will most likely continue to get along and find workable compromises. If, however, you differ on the role of God in your life, your moral values, or your methods of parenting, your relationship will be defined by conflict.

The fourth level is emotional intimacy. This is the level where you and your spouse give one another insight into who you are that no one else gets to see. It is where you share your dreams, your fantasies, your fears, the ridiculous ways you think and feel, and the things in your life of which you are most proud. This is the area where couples must be deliberate if they are going to make headway, because every step in this level of communication is vulnerable. Life will require you to communicate at the first three levels. You only reach level four if you choose to go there.

As you read the verses below, underline the kinds of words God doesn't want you to use as you communicate with your spouse.

"The lips of the righteous know what is appropriate, but the mouth of the wicked, only what is perverse" (Prov. 10:32).

"Coarse and foolish talking or crude joking are not suitable, but rather giving thanks" (Eph. 5:4).

"With it we bless our Lord and Father, and with it we curse men who are made in God's likeness. Out of the same mouth come blessing and cursing. My brothers, these things should not be this way" (Jas. 3:9-10).

Read Philippians 4:8 in your Bible. List the kinds of words that need to replace negative speech.

_____

_____

What is true and noble about your spouse?

_____

_____

What is lovely or admirable?

_____

_____

What is excellent or praiseworthy?

_____

_____

KEY WORDS

Often couples spend quite a bit of time talking to each other but still seem to hit stalemates in their communication. They want to connect, but in all their talking they don't know how to listen in a way that creates intimacy. We can all face this situation when we become slow communicators. We throw out hints rather than boldly tell our spouses how we are doing. As we learn to respond to these hints, we can encourage our spouses to reveal more of what is really going on in his or her heart.

When it comes to this type of disclosure, it has been our experience that people reveal themselves in stages. They start out with safe statements and progressively share more risky and vulnerable truths if the atmosphere of the conversation is conducive. We cannot discern motive unless the person shares and discloses it. We need to listen more and second-guess less. Too often we ask a question and then tune the person out while we rehearse our reply!

The key principle in promoting intimacy is giving permission to your spouse to share at a vulnerable level. If your spouse senses permission to share without being judged or prematurely "fixed," new information will emerge. This new information will lead you to a better understanding of what your spouse is all about at the emotional level that motivates actions and decisions. The skills that grant permission to your spouse are:

- Repeat key phrases the other person is saying. Key phrases usually have a feeling word in them. ("I am afraid we're getting into debt." "She upset me." "I am frustrated with him.") Look for the word or phrase that denotes a feeling and repeat that part of the sentence.
- Rephrase what has been said. ("What I hear you saying is …") Put what your spouse shared in your own words.
- Regroup. Ask for clarification. Is what you heard close to what he or she said? ("Am I in the ballpark?" or "Is this what you meant?")
- Reconnect. Try to relate his or her feelings to your own experience. ("Are you feeling a little like I felt when … ?") Try to compare something you have been through to something your spouse is trying to relate to you. The experience may be very different, but the feelings you experienced may be very similar.

Complete the following sentences.

I can tell my spouse is really listening to me when he or she …

_____

_____

My spouse can tell I'm really listening to him or her when I …

_____

_____

100 TO 1

One of the most powerful ways to rebuild open communication is to learn the art of being positive. Sometimes it isn't easy to discover ways to encourage a spouse. One woman came to me and said, "There is nothing here! No spark, no sizzle— nothing! I have no feelings. I want out of this marriage!"

I suggested we pray and ask God to show her one positive thing about her spouse. She went home and prayed some more. The next day she called me and said, "I thought of something."

"Good, what is it?" I asked hopefully.

"He's still here."

I thought she was kidding, but I could tell from her tone that she was completely serious.

"Okay, let's run with that. Let's brainstorm together ways you can tell him thanks for being there—but in a positive manner."

We made a list of several ways to positively say, "You're here!" and she began to use them. She would see her husband sitting in his recliner, remote in hand, watching sports. She'd walk by and rub his shoulders and say, "It's nice to know you're around."

She'd see him reading the paper and walk by and say, "It's nice to know I can count on some things in life—like you being here."

She came up with so many ways to positively say, "You're here, bud," that one day he got up out of that old recliner! He came into the living room where she was reading her Bible. He had never been interested in spiritual discussions before this, but he asked, "Honey, what are you reading?"

"My Bible. I am having a problem at work and this passage in Psalms is help-ing me."

"Why don't you read it to me?" he asked.

She did and added an explanation of how it applied to her life.

"That's pretty neat," he replied with genuine enthusiasm in his voice.

The next Sunday a miracle happened. Instead of going to his favorite chair, he asked if he could go to church with her—and he has been going ever since. In addi-tion, she now regularly tells me of his romantic gestures toward her.

She found the power of encouraging words by taking 100 percent of her energy and focusing it on one positive trait. Happiness and passion in marriage do not come from finding the right partner but in being the right partner—a positive partner!

Happiness and passion in marriage do not come from finding the right partner but in being the right partner.

Read the verses listed below in your Bible. Draw a line to match the reference to the kind of words that should be a priority in communicating with your spouse.

Proverbs 15:1	building
Proverbs 16:24	gentle
Ephesians 4:29	pleasant

"The LORD God said, 'It is not good for the man to be alone. I will make a helper who is like him.' This is why a man leaves his father and mother and bonds with his wife, and they become one flesh. Both the man and his wife were naked, yet felt no shame" (Gen. 2:18,24-25).

These verses depict the early foundation of marriage. Evaluate the foundations of your marriage. On each line, indicate whether you think that area of your marriage is strong or weak.

Companionship: How strong is your friendship?

weak

strong

Completeness: How well do you value each other's strengths and differences?

weak

strong

Connection: How well do you value each other's opinion?

weak

strong

Cleaving: How strongly is your marriage relationship a priority over every other relationship?

weak

strong

SPAGHETTI

Check the top three areas in which you think your husband is most successful. Compare your responses with his.

□ romance
□ sex
□ career
□ fatherhood
□ electronics

□ community involvement (coaching, clubs)
□ education/learning/schooling
□ home/yard/vehicle maintenance
□ church/spiritual growth
□ play (sports, hobbies, music)

List tasks you perform on a daily basis that you can do with ease while you're doing something else.

_____

_____

_____

Closeness: How would you rate your sex life?

weak

strong

Compare your responses. Brainstorm ways you can strengthen the weak areas.

1. Leah Ariniello, Gender and the Brain (Washington, DC: Society for Neuroscience, 1998), via ProQuest, an information service by Bell & Howell), quoted in Bill and Pam Farrel, Men Are Like Waffles—Women Are Like Spaghetti (Eugene, OR: Harvest House, 2001), 16.
2. Ibid.
3. Ibid, 17.
4. Malcolm Ritter, "Brains Differ in Navigation Skills," AP Science Writer, Tuesday, March 21, 2000, quoted in Bill and Pam Farrel, Why Men and Woman Act the Way They Do (Eugene, OR: Harvest House, 2003), 33.

WAFFLE

Check the top three things in which you feel most successful. Compare your responses with your wife.

☐ romance   ☐ community involvement (coaching, clubs)
☐ sex   ☐ education/learning/schooling
☐ career   ☐ home/yard/vehicle maintenance
☐ fatherhood   ☐ church/spiritual growth
☐ electronics   ☐ play (sports, hobbies, music)

What impresses you about how your wife handles the many tasks facing her each day?

_____

_____

_____

week two

Relaxing and De-stressing

Let us be concerned about one another
in order to promote love and good works.

Hebrews 10:24

Viewer Guide

"I've got gaps. She's got gaps. Together we fill gaps."
—Rocky Balboa as quoted by Bill Farrel

Passwords:

Passwords give you an opportunity to start a conversation over and get back on the same page.

Creating a password:

• Use _____ that is tied to a good memory.

• _____ on your password.

• Don't use passwords to avoid _____ _____.

Men and women relate differently.

Men and women relieve stress differently.

Stress:

Pick a code word.

Compliment instead of criticize.

When I (Pam) was a little girl, I used to spend summers on my grandparents' farm. My grandparents had a deep love for one another, but sometimes life's circumstances didn't go quite as anticipated. In those stressful moments, I witnessed coping patterns in my grandparents that worked quite well for them during their 60-plus years together.

A crisis would happen and almost instantaneously Grandma would begin to cook something—or at the very least clean something in the kitchen. She held back her tears, and sometimes her rage and anger, by cooking and cleaning. If my mother or any other woman was around, Grandma would start talking her way through the situation. And if no one was in sight, she would pick up the phone to chat. While she was working and talking, Grandpa quietly made his way to his shop. As a child I never understood why Grandpa wanted to spend so much time in that dirty shop. It reeked of oil and dust. Little did I realize this was a sanctuary for my grandfather's soul. While Grandma would cook and talk, Grandpa tinkered and created in his shop. Every kind of tool known to mankind was in that shop. He could stay out there all day because he had a little refrigerator and freezer packed with Grandma's prize-winning cookies.

If Grandpa stormed out to the shop angry, it magically calmed his frustrations and fears. As he worked, he would review, problem solve, and reflect on not only the problem but the people involved. In the shop he'd find his emotional center. But he would never confess that was what he was doing! He'd say he was "workin'." When Grandpa finally made his way back inside, the problem-solving conversations my grandparents had were in hushed, calm, and rational voices. Once they reached this point, their differences were quickly resolved.

We Process Stress Differently

We all get stressed. However, each gender handles stress differently. When stress hits, women need to traverse across all those noodles and emotionally connect to the people and situations associated with the problem at hand.

For this reason, talking is a huge help to a woman. As she talks through the stress of her life, the emotions associated with the circumstances dissipate. Solutions begin to emerge and simpler approaches appear as possibilities. It is as if stress catapults her into an emotional fog bank. Before she can navigate the course, she needs to clear the fog by talking her way through. Her conversational road map can include God, friends, extended family, and her husband. The combination of people she talks with may change with each situation, but she must talk her way out of stress.

Spaghetti, who do you talk to when you are stressed?

_____

Is your husband one of those people? ☒ yes ☒ no

Waffles, does your wife have anyone to talk to when she is stressed?
☒ yes ☒ no ☒ I have no idea.

Are you one of those people? ☒ yes ☒ no ☒ I hope not!

Compare your answers. Are you surprised? ☒ yes ☒ no

Explain. _____

_____

Men retreat to easy boxes in times of stress. Every man has certain boxes in his life that are much easier on him emotionally than others. When he enters these boxes, life melts away and he has an opportunity to recharge. Men do not get energized by constantly processing life. In fact, it drains them of energy. They get ready for the next challenge by disappearing into a stress-free box for a period of time. They emerge from that box energized, focused, and able to conquer the next obstacle.

Waffles, list your three favorite easy boxes where you go to de-stress.

1. _____

2. _____

3. _____

Spaghetti, what do you think are your husband's three favorite easy boxes in which to de-stress?

1. _____

2. _____

3. _____

Compare your answers. Are you surprised? ☒ yes ☒ no

Explain. _____

_____

How do we recognize a man's easy boxes? It seems God helped ladies out a bit with this one. Men's easy boxes are generally shaped like boxes. A newspaper is shaped like a box. A TV screen is shaped like a box. A basketball court and a football field are shaped like boxes. Mobile phones and computer screens are shaped like boxes. And the favorite of all men's safe, easy boxes—a bed—is shaped like a box!

Sleep and sex are two preferred coping mechanisms of the male gender, and of these two, sex is often a man's favorite easy box. If a man's life were pictured as a bingo card with all those rows of boxes, the sex box would be the free space in the center of the card. It is larger than all the other boxes, and a man can get there from pretty much every other box on the card!

COPING SKILLS

What is the first thing you normally do when you are stressed?

_____

"Draw near to God, and He will draw near to you" (Jas. 4:8).

According to this passage, what is the wisest first thing to do when you are stressed?

_____

Waffles, how might this change the easy box you go to?

_____

Spaghetti, how might this change the people you talk to or what you say?

_____

Go to God first. When stress feels like it is piling up inside you, go to God and unleash your fears and frustrations. Fear is often a component of the stress we experience. When we have no good way to calm fear, we further complicate the situation. Women typically express their feelings with more confrontational and hostile styles. Because women can become emotional under stress, it is easy for them to say and do things that exacerbate the problem rather than make it better. Words just roll out—hurtful words, heated words—and the damage that can be done should not be underestimated. Men, on the other hand, tend to turn their fear inward and put more stress on their bodies. As a result, "fear has been shown to contribute to more health problems in men than women."[1]

> Read the following verses from your Bible. What do you gain by
> going to God with your stresses?
>
> Psalm 18:2-3 _____
>
> Psalm 46:1 _____
>
> Proverbs 18:10 _____

God's shoulders are big enough to handle your deepest, darkest fears and frustrations. You don't have to worry about saying things you might never get back or that might wound God. He knows what you are feeling and thinking. By going to God first, you gain an emotional release and the clarity to think and talk things through.

Men, deliberately help your wife talk things out. The following approaches can help her talk through the anxiety of her current circumstances and bring her back to the woman you married.

1. Offer to listen. Say, "You seem pretty upset. Tell me what's going on."
2. Touch her. Gently pick up her hand, stroke her arm, wrap your arms around her. Start with a small amount of touch. If it calms her, give more.
3. Offer help. "Honey, what can I do to help?" "Do you want to take a minute and brainstorm what would help?" "Kids, let's pitch in and help Mom." These are all welcome phrases to a stressed-out woman.
4. Own up to it. If you are the problem because you broke a promise or dropped the ball on a responsibility, saying I'm sorry does help—especially when accompanied by numbers 1-3—and flowers! (And maybe a gift certificate!)

A woman will want to talk things out when she is under stress. She will instinctively seek out help. When one thing is wrong, everything feels wrong! When something is wrong, it is like a giant meatball has landed in the middle of her plate of spaghetti and noodles go flying everywhere! She will need to talk and talk until she has found a way to integrate the meatball into her noodles.

If something is wrong in a man's life, he wants to deal with it, stick the issue in one of those waffle boxes, put a lid on it, and nail it shut—never to be opened again. But women need to talk it through and talk it through and talk it through!

As his wife is talking it through, her husband is thinking, "I thought we talked about this!" You did! But she needs to talk it through until she feels comfortable with all the issues.

The challenge comes when you are the issue! This is the time to set your ego aside and patiently listen. Try not to react. If you'll let her noodle awhile on the issues, things will calm again and you'll look great in her eyes because you were the listening ear that helped her through.

Based on the following Scriptures, how would you describe a wise husband?

"The mind of a righteous person thinks before answering, but the mouth of the wicked blurts out evil things" (Prov. 15:28).

_____

"The one who gives an answer before he listens—this is foolishness and disgrace for him" (Prov. 18:13).

_____

"Everyone must be quick to hear, slow to speak, and slow to anger" (Jas. 1:19).

_____

Ladies, encourage your husband to spend time in easy boxes. Think of him like a battery. He needs to recharge. He can't keep processing life constantly like you can. He needs time in his favorite boxes to rest and recharge. When you look at a battery in a recharger, what does it look like it is doing? NOTHING!

Sometimes when he is on the computer or watching TV or tinkering it might seem like nothing to you, but it is something to him—it is recharging. Your husband needs time to get involved in mindless activity when stress hits your home. If you give him permission to go and are genuinely glad he has the opportunity, he will go without guilt and will be drawn toward you in the midst of the stress.

When stress hits a man's life, he may retreat to a favorite easy box. Women sometimes mistake this retreat for withdrawal, as if he doesn't care about what is happening in the family or marriage. However, the very opposite might be true. Studies say that when a marriage and family is under stress, men actually feel it at a deeper level. Instead of talking it out like women might, men often get quieter as they process, often "stuffing" their emotions.

Sometimes a woman gets angry when her husband retreats to the garage, TV, sports, or a hobby instead of interacting. Try not to take this personally. Men like to live in boxes they feel successful in and avoid those they do not feel successful in. If you want him to open up and share what is really going on, go into his favorite box with him and listen. Help him unpack his stress piece by piece. To do this you will need to slow down, quiet your opinions, and listen without reacting!

When we wrote Single Men Are Like Waffles–Single Women Are Like Spaghetti, we asked men and women what they appreciated about the opposite sex. The positive trait women named was: "Guys have the ability to shut down their emotions and handle the problem at hand." That's compartmentalizing at its best. Think of the video footage from 9-11 when the terrorists flew planes into the twin towers in New York City. The mayor was running for his own safety, knowing he had friends dying in that building but also knowing he needed to focus so more lives could be saved. While his heart was breaking, he set aside his own emotions for the greater public good, leading, handing out tasks, delegating—working tirelessly. That is the upside of compartmentalizing.

Read the following Proverbs.

"A foolish son is his father's ruin,
    and a wife's nagging is an endless dripping.
A house and wealth are inherited from fathers,
    but a sensible wife is from the Lord" (Prov. 19:13-14).

"Better to live in a wilderness
    than with a nagging and hot-tempered wife" (Prov. 21:19).

"Who can find a capable wife?
    She is far more precious than jewels.
The heart of her husband trusts in her,
    and he will not lack anything good.
She rewards him with good, not evil,
    all the days of her life" (Prov. 31:10-12).

How would you describe a wise wife?

_____

_____

COMPETING INTERESTS

What happens too often when a couple is under stress is that they compete for who gets to rest or relax first. (It may not be a conscious race, but when the pressure is building we all look for a way to relieve the stress.) A familiar scenario is a wife following her husband, chatting away while he is rushing to escape into the garage for some peace and quiet! No one's needs are getting met. When Bill and I were first married and we'd both had a rough day we'd ask, "Who's most stressed?" Bill might ask me, "Pam, do you need me to sit and listen before I go for a run?" Or I might ask Bill, "Do you need to go shoot some basketball?"

Asking the question showed we cared. Often just knowing your spouse cares, even though it doesn't solve the problem, makes things feel better.

Instead of fighting to make sure my need to de-stress came first, I found things generally got better at our home when I sent Bill off to shoot some hoops. While Bill was gone I would write out all my thoughts and feelings and pray through them. When Bill came home he was more relaxed and ready to listen, and I was less emotional and easier to listen to!

Read Proverbs 11:25 below.

"A generous man will prosper; he who refreshes others will himself be refreshed" (NIV).

What will happen if you generously seek to refresh your spouse?

_____

Have you personally experienced that truth? ☒ yes ☒ no

If so, briefly describe. _____

_____

WHAT I LOVE ABOUT YOU IS STRESSING ME!

The thing you first fell in love with when you met your spouse can also become a source of irritation over time. That strong trait that attracted you can also really bug you and tick you off! For example:

- You love the fact that your spouse is caring—until you have to share him or her with the whole world.

- You love your spouse's integrity until he or she is correcting your habits and choices.
- You love your mate's creativity until you can't find things in your home because they have been put away "creatively."
- You love his or her easygoing way until you realize you are the one making the majority of decisions or picking up around the house.
- You love that your spouse has a heart of compassion for animals or children until you realize your house has one too many pets or has become the teen hang out or unofficial childcare center.

Strength on one side, irritation on the other. Like two sides of the same coin, you need a way to flip the coin over and remember that's why you first fell in love.

This is a very common scenario played out by married couples. You married your spouse because being together addressed very significant needs in your life. You felt special, more complete. As a result, you were drawn close enough to take the big step of commitment and become husband and wife. Then the things you loved about your spouse appeared to change.

If you listen to these irritations and are willing to look beyond your anger to the qualities in your spouse that are so vital to your life, you will find you can build your marriage even when you're struggling. Your irritations can be the springboard to new conversations of intimacy.

To take advantage of the insight of your irritations, try the following:

1. Make a list of characteristics you appreciate most about your spouse. Keep this list in a place where you can review it often. Reminding yourself that you love your spouse is one of the best ways we know to lasso the whirlwind of modern life.
2. When you begin to get angry, ask yourself, "What did he or she say or do that has me so upset?" Something was done that triggered strong emotions in your soul. These strong emotions can either be seeds of anger or bridges of intimacy. If you can identify the trigger event, you can turn it to your advantage.
3. Ask yourself, "To which positive quality in my spouse's life is this irritation related?"
4. Repeat to yourself at least seven times, "I love my spouse for …" inserting the positive quality in his or her life that attracted you in the first place.

You've read the list. Now let's practice. First, list characteristics you appreciate about your spouse.

_____

_____

Now think about the last time you got irritated at your spouse.
What did your spouse say or do that irritated you?

_____

To what positive quality in your spouse's life is that irritation related?

_____

Now read that positive quality out loud seven times. (Yes, seven times!)

LISTEN TO YOUR PASSWORDS

Every couple gets in conversational binds from time to time. We all have sensitive emotional needs we have trouble managing. All couples have patterns in their relationship that are counterproductive to the growth of their marriage. When a couple gets stuck in these patterns or an emotional need sidetracks a conversation, it can be recaptured by using what we call passwords.

Passwords are words or phrases you and your spouse agree on that allow you to get back on track. They can be humorous or nostalgic statements that have special meaning to both of you. They remind you that your relationship is important and you are committed to making it work. They break the ice of stalemated conversations because you have agreed ahead of time that they will.

One of the greatest obstacles to marital intimacy for Blake and Jeannie was the habit Blake had of trying to fix Jeannie. She would share her concerns about various aspects of their life, and Blake would jump in and offer microwaved solutions. When he did this, she felt put down and heard messages from her past telling her she wasn't good enough. This became destructive to their marriage as she shifted into self-protection mode to fight off the perceived onslaught from Blake. They talked about a password they could use to remind them they really loved each other and wanted to connect.

Their solution was a stroke of genius. They both love the program "Home Improvement" and connect it with laughter and hope. They decided on the following password: "It looks like Tim Taylor has his toolbox out again." Jeannie had Blake's permission to use this anytime she felt he was trying to fix her. If she felt the feelings of low self-esteem or anger coming to the surface, she could lovingly look into Blake's eyes and use their password. This would cause Blake to stop and think about the effect he was having on his wife. Blake also had permission to use this phrase when he sensed he was trying to fix the situation and Jeannie was feeling run over in the process. Since they both agreed to incorporate the password there has been more laughter in their home, and there has also been a greater degree of understanding between them. They now have a way of interrupting conversations that had historically gone awry. They no longer sit around after an argument wondering what happened.

The danger of passwords is the temptation to manipulate your spouse. If he or she is upset, you might be tempted to use your password to force your spouse to be "more reasonable" and see things your way. You may also be tempted to throw your password in his or her face to end conversations that are unpleasant but necessary to the health of your marriage. Passwords must be used with compassion and an honest desire to build a healthier relationship.

Brainstorm two or three passwords that might break tense communication moments in your marriage.

1. _____

2. _____

3. _____

Compare your passwords with those your spouse creates. Together agree upon one password you will use to get sensitive conversations back on track.

Our agreed upon password: _____

_____

Get Away from It All

Everyone needs tools to lower stress: understanding gender differences, learning to use passwords, and remembering why you first fell in love are all safeguards to your love. But one of the best ways to protect your love (and your life) is to make sure you get some alone time as a couple.

Taking a step back can help you gain rest, perspective, and a second wind. Any stress is easier to go through when you are emotionally connected as a couple. Getting away does two things: it shrinks a woman's world (less noodles to deal with), and it is a favorite coping strategy of men—retreat, relax, and reconnect. Depending on the stress and circumstances, different kinds of getaways are in order.

What is your honest attitude about resting? Check all that apply.

☒ What is it? ☒ It's a waste.

☒ It's not possible. ☒ I feel guilty about resting.

☒ I love it! ☒ It is good to schedule it regularly.

☒ Other: _____

Look up each of the following verses in your Bible. What do each have to say about resting?

Genesis 2:2-3 _____

Exodus 34:21 _____

THE GREAT GETAWAY

Sometimes getting away is the best way to romance your mate. Guys, plan a weekend away when she can talk and talk and talk. By listening, you'll sweep her off her feet. Let her shop a little and pick up a few things for the kids and you'll be a hit.

Ladies, plan a weekend away where you never leave the hotel room and you'll be a hit! Or at least keep the expectation low: golf, dinner, sex; sporting event, dinner, sex—get the drift?

THE R AND R GETAWAY

Time off for rest and relaxation. Time to do absolutely nothing. Lie in the sun, read novels, slow down. Couples who live a fully packed, fast-paced life are wise to build these breaks into their schedules on a regular basis.

Bill and I aim for a 24-hour oasis quarterly. Sometimes scheduling every aspect of life is what has you down, so be spontaneous. Pack a toothbrush, some lingerie, and a bathing suit and head out! Let your whims carry you.

• Flip a coin to decide left or right; north or south.

• Choose a city and go to the tourist bureau or Chamber of Commerce to see what the most unique, most economical accommodations might be.

• Pretend to kidnap your sweetheart. Call ahead and book appointments under a false name with his or her secretary. Then walk in with a blindfold and steal your love away to some surprise getaway location.

• Leave your watches at home. Sleep when you're tired; eat when you're hungry.

• Go on an off day. Often Tuesday through Thursday is less expensive in tourist towns, and weekends can be less expensive at hotels that cater to business clientele.

A PLANNED GETAWAY

Once a year Bill and I set aside time away to talk over the business side of life. We set goals, talk finances, plan for the children's needs, and do calendaring and scheduling for the year. This alleviates many arguments because we are both operating off the same agenda. We discuss expectations we have of each other. We talk over career plans, business items, pace of life—anything that either of us sees as a challenge to overcome.

By taking these regular planning getaways, we keep our other getaways free from distractions so we can really enjoy each other rather than have the mood ruined by a business item.

THE SURPRISE GETAWAY

We "plan" our surprises! That is, on each other's birthdays we seek to do something out of the ordinary. Take turns planning your getaways so that one of you is always surprised. These take a lot of preparation on the part of the one doing the "whisking" and a lot of flexibility on the part of the one being "whisked."

THE UN-GETAWAY

This is the most creative and easiest getaway to make a regular part of your lifestyle. These are the quick overnighters when the kids go away for the night and you make your place an instant hotel. This idea takes away the excuse, "We can't afford it." Even a night curled up together on the sofa, watching a romantic movie, followed by a morning of sleeping in can be welcome relief for busy couples.

THE BUILDING GETAWAY

This is for marriage tune-ups and enrichment. If you build into your love life before the crisis hits, you'll find that no crisis can tear you apart! The key to a healthy marriage-building getaway is to choose positive input. Choose one that values commitment, a couple's uniqueness, and includes information and exercises to build a couple's spiritual, emotional, and physical life.

We recommend a marriage renewal event at least once a year. When a marriage begins, you enter with a level of relational skills, then year upon year the level of responsibility rises. Most couples make the mistake of thinking the level of relational skills they had when they married is enough to carry them through life. Nothing could be farther from the truth! The best way to stay connected emotionally and to ensure happiness for a lifetime is to build new relational skills into your love year upon year.[2]

Stress will most certainly be an active part of your life together, but stress does not need to be devoid of hope. If you provide ample opportunities for discussion and time spent in easy boxes, you will discover that everything in your life can bring you closer to each other.

"I am at rest in God alone;
my salvation comes from Him."
Psalm 62:1

According to Psalm 62:1. What is ultimately your only source of rest?

_____

SPAGHETTI "Come away, my lover" (Song of Songs 8:14).

Which of the getaways listed in this week's study was most appealing to

you? _____

What can you do to make this getaway with your husband happen?

_____

List some activities you would enjoy doing with your husband that would allow him to relax and you to talk. Compare your list with your husband's and determine at least one activity you will do this month.

_____

_____

How will you personally rest in God this week?

_____

_____

How can you and your spouse rest in God together this week?
☒ attend a Christian concert
☒ sit quietly next to each other and listen to a worship CD
☒ take a walk on a nature trail
☒ other: _____

1. Daniel J. Canary and Tara M. Emmers-Sommer with Sandra Faulkner, Sex and Gender Differences in Personal Relationships (New York: Guilford Press, 1997), 31.
2. For information on marriage enrichment events, visit www.lifeway.com/marriage.

WAFFLE

"Come away, my lover" (Song of Songs 8:14).

Which of the getaways listed in this week's study was most appealing to

you? _____

What can you do to make this getaway with your wife happen?

_____

List some activities you would enjoy doing with your wife that would allow her to talk and you to relax. Compare your list with your wife's and determine at least one activity you will do this month.

_____

_____

week three
Living and Loving

Encourage each other daily,
while it is still called today,
so that none of you is
hardened by sin's deception.

Hebrews 3:13

Viewer Guide

Romance is the practical outworking of encouragement.

The biblical definition of encouragement:

Encourage each other through:

• Physical touch

• Encouraging words

Two ways to get encouraging words into your relationship:

1. _____

2. _____

Encourage each other through developing your creativity:

1. _____

2. _____

3. _____

4. _____

Romance is one of the many practical ways you can encourage your spouse. We are called in Hebrews 3:13 to "encourage each other daily, while it is still called today, so that none of you is hardened by sin's deception." The word encourage literally means "called alongside to help." When you encourage your spouse, you are committing yourself to help in whatever way you can. Sometimes it means cheerleading, sometimes it means confronting, sometimes it means flirting, and sometimes it means romancing.

Romance is a skill. Like any skill, romance can seem awkward in the beginning. Romance is a lot like driving. When you first started to drive, you drove with both hands at the 10 and 2 position. But the more you drove, the more comfortable you became. Now you can drive with one hand while eating a hamburger, tuning your radio, and talking on your cell phone. The more you practice romance, the more romantic you are!

Romance is knowing your lover. Different personalities prefer different types of romance. But we often expect our mates to love to be loved the way we feel loved. What's romantic to us should to be romantic to them, right? Wrong!

Romance to Her

To a woman, romance is when her man ties different aspects of her life together. If Bill calls me on Tuesday and asks me to go out on Friday, I get a card in the mail on Wednesday saying, "Can't wait 'til the weekend!" On Thursday he asks me to wear the cute little black dress he loves. On Friday flowers are delivered with a card, "See ya soon!" He picks me up and takes me to places I told him I wanted to go, and we do things I said I wanted to do. At the restaurant there is a gift—already in place— and then on Monday I get a card in the mail that says, "Thanks for a great evening!"

Wow! I am swept off my feet! (He gets bonus points if he arranged child care!) He has tied nearly a week together in a romantic memory. Guys, if you take time to tie many romantic details together like this, the aura of it can last years!

Read Song of Songs 2:10-14. How did the husband romance his wife? _____

_____

_____

Romance to Him

Romancing men is pretty simple. Have clear expectations and stick to them! If you say you're going to dinner and a movie, stick to that. Don't think your husband should automatically know you want to take a walk after the movie and talk about hopes and dreams. To really romance a guy, connect some of his favorite easy boxes. If I want to romance Bill, I get tickets to a football game, take him to his favorite restaurant, and take him home for great sex. In fact, he'd give you the tickets to the game and skip dinner if he knew for sure there would be sex. Bingo!

Read Song of Songs 1:2-4. How did the wife romance her husband?

_____

_____

How well do you know your lover? Read the descriptions of the four types of lovers on the chart[1] on pages 44-45. See if you can pick yourself out, and see if you can discern which type of lover you are married to.

My romantic personality: _____

My spouse's romantic personality: _____

Read Philippians 2:3-4 below. Underline what these verses say you should do if your romantic personality and preferences differ from your spouse's.

"Do nothing out of rivalry or conceit, but in humility consider others as more important than yourselves. Everyone should look out not [only] for his own interests, but also for the interests of others" (Phil. 2:3-4).

The Hopeless Romantic

EXAMPLES
Anne of Avonlea, Cupid

CHARACTERISTICS

people-oriented	extroverted	fun
unique	daring	active
center of attention	enjoys new adventures	exotic

PREFERENCES IN ROMANCE
1. Anything new
2. Entertainment that is personal and touches the heart
3. Human drama (plays, musicals, concerts, sporting events)
4. Adventurous outings
5. Exotic getaways

PERSONALITY TYPE: Sanguine; Inspirational; Otter

Wind Beneath My Wings

EXAMPLES
Superman, Robert and Elizabeth Browning

CHARACTERISTICS

people-oriented	introverted	relaxed
adaptable	stress free	has time to talk
reliable	compassionate	nurturing
	consistent	

PREFERENCES IN ROMANCE
1. Light schedule
2. Simple activities
3. Time to relax
4. Escape from reality
5. Entertainment when there is plenty of time to enjoy it

PERSONALITY TYPE: Phlegmatic; Steady; Retriever

Knight in Shining Armor; Queen of Hearts

EXAMPLES

Lancelot, James Bond, Robin Hood, Crocodile Dundee, Joan of Arc, Lois Lane

CHARACTERISTICS

dominant	task-oriented	extroverted
loves new experiences	controlling	focused
cooperative	decisive	active

PREFERENCES IN ROMANCE

1. Adventurous activity (if in charge)
2. Club Med
3. Hiking
4. Anything they decide is a good idea

PERSONALITY TYPE: Choleric; Dominant; Lion

True Blue Lover

EXAMPLES

Jane Eyre, Romeo and Juliet

CHARACTERISTICS

task-oriented	introverted	predictable
scheduled	creative	practical
orderly	sensitive	persistent
	enjoys things that are significant	

PREFERENCES IN ROMANCE

1. Guided tours
2. Educational outings
3. Museums
4. Historical tours
5. Long conversations

PERSONALITY TYPE: Melancholy; Cautious; Beaver

Spice It Up!

Can your marriage continue to sizzle like it did when you were dating? How can you add a little zip to your love life? You can continue dating throughout your lives. However, couples often complain that life and love become mundane and routine with each passing year. It doesn't have to be that way! Try these relationship enhancers to put the spark back in your love life.

Look back. Try a date that revisits early memories of your life together. Take a trip to the place you first met, first kissed, or where your marriage proposal took place. If finances or distance are a concern, plan a picnic and bring a photo album of the early years and reminisce. Play "your" song while taking a drive to your old neighborhood, high school, college, or favorite restaurant. Maybe this is the year to renew your vows or write new vows for the next decade. Looking back can help reestablish those feelings that first drew you together, and it can remind you both of all the years of memories you have invested in each other.

Make a list of things you did together when you first fell in love.

_____

_____

_____

Schedule one of those activities for this week.

We will do _____

on _____ .

Look ahead. Bill and I each keep a list of dream dates we'd like to go on. Once a year we give our lists to each other. We also give each other a "love list" of at least 10 things that cost nothing but make us feel loved. Having these lists helps us surprise each other on a regular basis. You can also invest in your marriage by attending a marriage seminar, conference, or retreat. You may choose to invest in your relationship by purchasing a gift that says, "I love the person you are becoming. I'm excited about your life—and ours. Just wanted you to know I believe in your dream." When a couple invests in one another's dreams and plans for the transitions of life, they gain the ability to fall in love over and over again.

Answer this question: If I could go anyplace in the world on a romantic rendezvous with my spouse, where would I want to go and why?

_____

_____

List five dates you'd love to go on with your spouse this year.

1. _____

2. _____

3. _____

4. _____

5. _____

Set aside one hour today and do something fun as you talk about dream dates together (take a walk, snuggle, have a milk shake with two straws).

Seize the moment. Invest in the now. Practice the art of touch. Reach over and hold his hand, give her a squeeze, pat him on the back. With all the technology available today, there are plenty of ways to reach out and touch the one you love. Leave a message on voicemail, fax a love note, or e-mail a missive that is filled with symbols and word pictures only the two of you will understand. Stop by home or your spouse's office just to whisper, "I love you" and then drop a single rose as you leave. Or call your mate and read a few verses from the Song of Songs over the phone.

Make a list of free things that express love to you (examples: when he takes out the trash without being asked, when she massages your shoulders at the end of a long day).

_____

_____

_____

Romance doesn't have to take a lot of money, just a little bit of time spent thinking about your mate.[2] It isn't about the money—it really is the thought that counts! The gift your spouse most enjoys is you!

The gift your spouse most enjoys is you!

Encouragement Can Be Romantic

You can do a lot to encourage your mate. Trust and emotional safety build creativity. Over the next few days, listen for an area of insecurity in your spouse. Maybe she is a little anxious about her weight, or he is a little melancholy over his fading youth. Make a list of ways you can praise or encourage the one you love in that area of insecurity. Then prepare a "gift of praise" designed to encourage. It could be something you say, something you do, or a tangible gift. The key is to focus on the one you love.

Read the verses below.

"The local people showed us extraordinary kindness" (Acts 28:2).

"Listen, for I speak of noble things, and what my lips say is right.
For my mouth tells the truth, and wickedness is detestable to my lips.
I possess good advice and competence; I have understanding and
strength" (Prov. 8:6-7,14).

"Anxiety in a man's heart weighs it down, but a good word cheers
it up" (Prov. 12:25).

List ways you will encourage your mate by:

extending an extraordinary kindness

_____

speaking noble, right, and truthful words

_____

offering your competence, strength, or understanding

_____

cheering up with a good word, gift, or date

_____

Perplexing Passion[3]

Sex is one of the greatest yet most awkward activities in which husbands and wives engage. A successful sexual encounter will leave a man and his wife relaxed, satisfied, and thrilled to be in love. A couple who is in sync with each other sexually will be more confident, think more clearly, and be more willing to sacrifice themselves for the good of the relationship. Sadly, few couples experience a satisfying sexual relationship on a regular basis.

This is a complex and highly emotional issue, but there is hope that every couple can gain enough insight into the sexual dance of marriage to have a long-term, fulfilling intimate life. The keys to great sex are accepting that men and women are different sexually, valuing your spouse's sexual response as much as your own, and committing yourself to the behaviors that meet your spouse's sexual needs.

Let's look at what God says about sex. Read Genesis 1:28 in your Bible. What is the first, and most obvious, reason God created sex?

_____

Procreation: Sex creates babies. For the human race to go forward, sex has to take place. Genesis 4 is a difficult story of the betrayal between Cain and Abel and the subsequent murder of Abel. But in the midst of the story, sex is referred to as knowing one's spouse intimately: "Adam knew his wife Eve intimately, and she conceived and gave birth to Cain. … Cain knew his wife intimately, and she conceived and gave birth to Enoch. … Adam knew his wife intimately again, and she gave birth to a son and named him Seth" (Gen 4:1,17,25). Having kids is a nice result of a good sex life.

Proclamation: When a couple marries, their act of consummation is a symbolic picture of the wedding of Christ and His church. In a real sense, each time a couple enjoys each other sexually, it is a proclamation to Satan that God's plan of love will win out over Satan's misguided attempt to dethrone the Lord in the garden of Eden.

Read Ephesians 5:28-32. What did Paul use to illustrate the love

between Christ and His church? _____

Check the areas of intimacy you believe are conveyed by the phrase "become one flesh."

☒ physical   ☒ social   ☒ emotional   ☒ spiritual

Reconnection: Life is busy, but God planted a yearning in the human soul to be together. The deep intellectual, emotional, and spiritual connection that happens during sex is progressive. Good sex makes us yearn for more good sex. A wonderful cycle of marital union can develop which will keep a couple coming back together over and over.

According to 1 Corinthians 7:1-5, what is an assumed regular

activity of marriage?_____

What is the only reason Paul said a husband and wife should

refrain from sexual intimacy?_____

Who decides if the couple won't engage in sexual intimacy for a period of time?

☒ the husband   ☒ the wife
☒ the mother-in-law   ☒ the husband and wife together

Recreation: God thinks sex should be fun. In the Old Testament, when a king spotted Isaac and Rebekah caressing in a private moment the wording he used to describe their activity is "sporting with" (Gen 26:8, KJV). That sounds like fun to us! In Song of Songs, you see the king and his newlywed wife are enjoying their relationship immensely.

Rejuvenation: Sex within the context of marriage is good for your emotional and physical well-being. Sex raises the endorphin level, making you happier. While doing research for our marriage books, we have been amazed at the number of journal articles that make the case that the best sex and the happiest people are those in long-term marriages! Sex is like the battery that keeps a marriage going strong year after year. Your marriage might survive for the long haul without much sex, but it won't be near the fun. Do yourself and your spouse a favor and energize your marriage with regular sex. You might discover you are healthier and happier!

"Marriage is honorable among all, and the bed undefiled; but fornicators and adulterers God will judge" (Heb. 13:4, NKJV).

Based on Hebrews 13:4, circle how God regards sexual intimacy between a husband and wife. Underline how you regard your own sex life with your spouse.

honorable   horrible   hilarious   happy

For more biblical perspectives on this gift of sexual intimacy, read the following passages from the Song of Songs and note ways sexual love is expressed between husband and wife.

1:2 _____

2:6 _____

2:8-9 _____

7:8-13 _____

If Only You Could Know What I Know

Men and women approach sex differently. Most men would like their wives to be more aggressive in their intimate encounters and most women would like their husbands to slow down and be more understanding of their emotional needs. This tension exists because husbands and wives have been wired differently by their Creator in the realm of sexual pleasure. As a result, an intimate relationship is an ongoing journey of discovery.

Read Proverbs 5:15-19. What is essential to a growing sexual relationship between a husband and wife?

_____

Read Proverbs 5:20-23. Why must you daily accept God's challenge to grow in your sexual relationship with your spouse?

_____

Proverbs 5 recognizes the consistent temptation to wander to sexual experiences that are inherently unhealthy. The path away from this temptation is a commitment to a lifelong, intimate marriage. And don't just be faithful to your spouse—enjoy your marriage and take pleasure in making love to your mate!

WHAT A WOMAN REALLY WANTS BEHIND CLOSED DOORS

Men, your wife's sexual fulfillment is connected to everything else in her life. When she feels close to you emotionally, she is more responsive. When she is in touch with her children and proud of how you father them, she is more attracted to you. When her career is moving forward and you are supportive of her pursuits, she finds you more irresistible. The more you are a part of her life, the stronger her desire for you is.

Every month she is reminded of her reproductive potential as she goes through her menstrual cycle. Much of her menstrual cycle is uncomfortable and inconvenient. She has no choice but to experience this cycle every month. Some days she feels very sexy and interested in intimate contact with you. On other days, she is out of sorts even though she tries not to be.

There is a remarkable benefit to the way women are created. It takes more for her to reach arousal, but when things are right she can experience pleasure much longer and more intensely than her husband. God intended that sexual pleasure be a normal part of a woman's life. When a man commits himself to his wife's sexual fulfillment, a fascinating dynamic takes place. She will experience pleasure more often and he will have his ego boosted because he feels like a better lover.

SEX IN THE BOX

The simplest way to understand a man's sex drive is to picture it in the center box of his waffle. As we mentioned earlier, this box is bigger than any of the others and can be entered from any other box. The reason this box is bigger is that it has compartments in it. Since men are focused on sex much more than women, it is easy to conclude they have a single-minded approach to sexual activity. In reality there are three independent forces that drive a man's desire: a reproductive mandate, sexual tension, and intimacy.

Reproductive mandate: God created mankind for survival. To ensure its success, God built into the human species characteristics that constantly encourage sexual activity. Men are visually stimulated. It has been this way from the beginning of creation. When God created Eve, Adam was so taken by her appearance that he spontaneously broke out in song. "This is now bone of my bones and flesh of my flesh; she shall be called 'woman,' for she was taken out of man" (Gen. 2:23, NIV).

The intention of the original plan was to give each man eyes to admire his wife throughout their life together. The intensity of a man's ability to notice women was given to him so his wife would be attractive to him all the days of his life.

Sexual tension: The second compartment of the sex box has to do more with stress than intimacy. When a man becomes sexually active, his body adjusts to an anticipated schedule of intercourse. But no couple ever stays "on schedule," and that is where the tension builds.

For most men, this is where the tyranny of sex shows up. When he is not able to have sex "on schedule," he experiences a number of physiological and emotional reactions. He finds himself staring at his wife more as her features intensify in his mind. He longs to be with her as her features look more attractive to him. As time goes by, he becomes irritable, even unreasonable. The whole time he is saying to himself, Get a grip. You are stronger than this. It won't hurt to wait. But no amount of reasoning reduces the tension he feels in his body.

This struggle is intensified if stress is high. As stress increases in a man's life, his awareness of the tension in his body is heightened. The experience of sex relieves the tension in his body and transports him mentally and emotionally into the box of sexual expression. When he enters that box, all the cares of his life are put on hold. The fact that good sex is usually followed by sleep only adds to the impact sexual activity has in relieving stress in his life.

The average man would like to be able to turn this part of his sex drive off. It is persistent and unyielding. The tension builds involuntarily and consumes much more of his life than he is comfortable with. He also has no idea how to explain this issue to his wife. Every man longs for his wife to be understanding of this struggle because he is bound to live with it. When she is sensitive and compassionate about the constant intensity of his sex drive, he is amazed and falls in love with her over and over again. When she is critical of it or insensitive, he turns inward and silently fights the struggle alone.

How is the sexual tension that exists in all marriages displayed

in Song of Songs 5:2-6? _____

How do you feel to discover that even these biblical lovers weren't always "in the mood" at the same time? Check all that apply.

☒ relieved   ☒ surprised   ☒ puzzled

☒ vindicated   ☒ reassured   ☒ frustrated

Desire for intimacy: The third compartment of a man's sex box is the one women find attractive. A man does not love sex just because of what it does physically. He also longs to be significantly connected to the love of his life. He wants to know his wife, and he wants to be known by her. He longs for the safe haven of a loving marriage just as she does.

Sacrificing to please your spouse sexually is a mature gift of love. The Apostle Paul explained God's picture of true unity: "Do nothing out of rivalry or conceit, but in humility consider others as more important than yourselves. Everyone should look out not [only] for his own interests, but also for the interests of others. Make your own attitude that of Christ Jesus" (Phil. 2:3-5).

Read Galatians 5:13-15 below.

"You are called to freedom, brothers; only don't use this freedom as
an opportunity for the flesh, but serve one another through love.
For the entire law is fulfilled in one statement: You shall love your
neighbor as yourself. But if you bite and devour one another,
watch out, or you will be consumed by one another" (Gal. 5:13-15).

When it comes to sexual intimacy how can you:

serve your spouse?_____

love your spouse?_____

not use your spouse? _____

Set Boundaries to Protect Your Love

A question we are often asked is, "What is okay in the bedroom?" Let us summarize three main guidelines on what God says. Sex should be:

Done out of love, never forced. Very little is said in the Bible in the way of rules. There are more principles like: all lovemaking should be in a committed relationship of marriage (1 Thess. 4:3; Heb. 13:4); each person should honor and respect the other (Eph. 5); and our character should reflect Christ's with an other focus and a heart of love that wants the best for our mates (Phil. 2).

Agreed upon. "Diligently keeping the unity of the Spirit with the peace that binds [us]" (Eph. 4:3). "Above all, [put on] love—the perfect bond of unity" (Col. 3:14).

According to Ephesians 4:3 and Colossians 3:14, what should be the guiding principle and priority in the sexual life of your marriage? Underline your answer.

personal satisfaction   unity

spouse's satisfaction   excitement

No sexual act, no matter how much it is desired by one should be forced on the other. A couple who wants to enjoy a lifetime of sexual satisfaction will seek to grow in their intimate expression to one another but will only engage in activities that are mutually agreed upon. Anything less will rob you of the very pleasure you are seeking.

On the flip side, make sure your resistance is based on Scripture and not past baggage, a poor self-image, or an untrue view of what God blesses in marriage. If you are in doubt, pray it out. God will show you how to respond to your mate. God loves you both and wants you both to be fulfilled. Check your attitude. Try not to rob your mate of an experience for your convenience or because you feel out of your comfort zone. Consider giving your mate the gift of experiencing something he or she has asked for, especially if there is no clear Scripture against it.

Is there anything you have been demanding or refusing in your marital sexual life that is undermining unity in your marriage?
☒ yes ☒ no ☒ I'm not sure.

Talk about this with God first. Then talk to your mate.

Just the two of you. This should be obvious, but let's make sure we're clear: God forbids mate swapping, multiple partners, phone or cybersex with anyone other than a marriage partner, and pornography. Hebrews 13:4 gives the clear guideline: "Marriage must be respected by all, and the marriage bed kept undefiled, because God will judge immoral people and adulterers." Sex is a bond meant for only the two of you. You can protect your love for one another by establishing boundaries.

Read the following passages and determine how each can help you establish healthy boundaries in your relationship.

Proverbs 4:20-23 _____

Philippians 4:4-7 _____

Boundaries Build Trust

Bill and I have some pretty tight boundaries that guard our relationships with the opposite sex. We are never alone with a person of the opposite sex in a counseling setting. We never dine with someone of the opposite sex alone, nor do we travel alone with a member of the opposite sex. We even make a practice of dropping off those of the opposite sex before we take home those of the same sex in a carpool situation. But more important than these structural boundaries, we have emotional boundaries. We do not share with others what our spouse should hear first. Our deepest sorrows and greatest thrills are not shared with anyone until first shared with each other.

But the boundary that protects our love more than any other is the choice to walk away from any relationship in which we are feeling sexual attraction toward a member of the opposite sex—and we tell each other we've made that choice.

What boundaries have you established in your marriage?

_____

_____

_____

_____

_____

If you have not established any boundaries, set aside time this week for you and your spouse to establish protective boundaries for your relationship.

CULTIVATE A SENSE OF HUMOR

Because sex is so intense, every couple experiences times of awkwardness in addition to times of satisfying intimacy. All these experiences create a legacy of sexual love in your relationship. Your ability to meet one another's needs along with your ability to laugh together at your times of awkwardness will continually add value to your love.

One couple with a fourth grade son was having difficulty finding time to enjoy one another sexually. Their careers were in full swing, their son was very energetic, and they were very involved in their church. Out of desperation they came up with what they thought was a great idea. They told their son, "John, we've got a new game for you to play. From our balcony you can see most of the neighborhood. What would you think about playing detective by standing on the balcony and calling out what people are doing?"

Being a curious boy, John enthusiastically agreed. Mom and Dad thought they would be able to steal away to their bedroom and enjoy each other while John was announcing the activity of the neighborhood. As they settled into bed they began to hear their son.

"Two boys are riding by on bicycles. Mr. Kennedy is taking out the trash. I wonder if he has any top secrets he is throwing away. I see a kid on a skateboard. Four girls are skipping rope."

The parents thought everything was going smoothly when John announced, "The Andersons are having sex."

They bolted up and shouted, "How do you know they are having sex?"

John replied, "Their kids are on the balcony, too!"

We hope our kids see your kids on the balcony real soon.

1. For more on personalities: Florence Littauer, Marita Littauer, Getting Along with Almost Anybody: The Complete Personality Book (Grand Rapids: Fleming H. Revell, 1998); Jim and Suzette Brawner, Taming the Family Zoo: Maximizing Harmony and Minimizing Family Stress (Colorado Springs: NavPress, 1998); and Bob Phillips, The Delicate Art of Dancing with Porcupines: Learning to Appreciate the Finer Points of Others (Ventura, CA: Regal Books, 1989).
2. For a free list of inexpensive dating ideas, visit : http://love-wise.com/articles.php.
3. For more information about sexual relationships between married couples, read Bill and Pam Farrel, Red-Hot Monogamy: Making Your Marriage Sizzle (Eugene, OR: Harvest House, 2006).

SPAGHETTI "He is absolutely desirable. This is my love, and this is my friend" (Song of Songs 5:16).

Read Song of Songs 5:9-16.

This week, how will you let your husband know:

he is desirable? _____

_____

he is better than anyone else to you? _____

_____

he is your love and your friend? _____

_____

In all honesty, how comfortable do you feel with the topic of romancing your husband? Mark your response on the line below.

not at all

I love romance!

Compare your response with your husband's.

Do you both feel the same way about romance? q yes q no

Pray together, thanking God for the gifts of romance and sexual intimacy.

Ask Him to help you and your husband appreciate and make full use of those gifts.

"How delightful your love is … my bride" (Song of Songs 4:10).

WAFFLE

Read Song of Songs 4:1-11.

This week, how will you let your wife know:

she is beautiful? _____

_____

she has captured your heart? _____

_____

you delight in her love? _____

_____

In all honesty, how comfortable do you feel with the topic of romancing your wife? Mark your response on the line below.

not at all

I love romance!

Compare your response with your wife's.

Do you both feel the same way about romance? q yes   q no

Pray together, thanking God for the gifts of romance and sexual intimacy.

Ask Him to help you and your wife appreciate and make full use of those gifts.

week four
HandlingConflict

Put on heartfelt compassion, kindness, humility, gentleness, and patience, accepting one another and forgiving one another … Just as the Lord has forgiven you, so also you must [forgive].

Colossians 3:12-13

Viewer Guide

The most important skill a married couple can learn is forgiveness.

Forgiveness is not:

-
-
-
-
-

Forgiveness is:
- a choice of your will to not allow anyone to control your emotional well-bring except for God.
- a private, vertical act between you and God.

Reconciliation is a horizontal act between two people.

The Six Statements of Forgiveness:

1. _____
2. _____
3. _____
4. _____
5. _____
6. _____

Differences between genders accompanied by differences in personality, layered with differences in your family of origin or past emotional baggage all combine to guarantee that every couple will experience conflict. You will disagree with one another; you will argue with one another; and you will irritate one another. But conflict doesn't have to be destructive to the relationship. Conflict can heighten your understanding of what is really important in your relationship if you know how to make it work for you rather than against you.

Both men and women experience periods of dissatisfaction in their relationships. While they experience distress for similar reasons, they process disappointments in different ways. Wives complain and criticize more than their husbands.[1] Because a woman's life is made up of connections, she feels the stress of discord. Her first instinct is to talk through it, and when the atmosphere turns negative it makes sense to her to express the negative emotions she is feeling. Often her distressed words force the couple to discuss subjects which otherwise would be avoided.

When conflict arises, the husband's first reaction is often fear of failure. His confidence about conflict resolution is usually not as high as his wife's. He has been outtalked by her many times, and he has received "the look" even more often. "The look" is a very useful tool for women and can accomplish many objectives. When she is upset with her husband, "the look" will often get him to stop whatever it is he is doing. When she is disappointed in his behavior, "the look" can spur him to action that is more pleasing to her. When her kids are out of line, "the look" can bring them into compliance with the plan quicker than anything Dad can do. We have seen men try to use "the look," but it is comical. "The look" must have been attached to the rib that Adam passed on to Eve.

Because men often get outplayed in the conflict game, husbands present more excuses than their wives and withdraw emotionally more often.[2]

Win/Win Propositions

Research shows that men like to compete. When physical or chaotic situations present themselves, men respond with a call to action. They feel the need to win by conquering the challenge. Sports, money challenges, a dare from a friend, or a necessary project all fit the bill. Women also feel the need to compete, but in an entirely different way. When the relationships of her life are out of order, she feels the call to action. A wife will use competitive tactics when the conflict involves the development or maintenance of key relationships.[3] It has also been shown that women will experience anger when they are faced with uncontrollable situations such as snowstorms or emotional deadlocks.[4]

Successful couples learn the secret
of fighting for their relationship rather
than fighting against one another.

Read Colossians 3:12-13 on page 60. What attitudes are necessary
if a husband and wife are going to fight for their relationship rather
than with each other?

_____

_____

What actions are necessary?

_____

_____

Pause and pray, asking for forgiveness for times you have not
displayed these attitudes or actions with your spouse. Ask for the
spirit of humility to accept God's Word about conflict and forgiveness in this week's study and for God to use this study to help you
handle conflict positively.

CONFLICT COVENANT

One of the best ways to have peace in the home is to avoid conflict by taking
preventative measures. Knowing what to do with your anger is a good place to
begin. We are all imperfect. We all make mistakes or have personality quirks that
frustrate our mates. What can you do with your own anger when something in
your mate really makes you mad?

Read Proverbs 14:16; 15:1,18; 29:11 from your Bible. On the chart at the
top of page 64, list negative and positive ways to handle anger.

Negative	Positive

Circle the words and phrases in each column that best describe
how you handle your anger with your spouse.

When things heat up and issues come to the surface, the way you handle the issues as a couple can either make things better or much worse. We have found that couples who have some "rules of engagement," or what we call a Conflict Covenant, handle issues in a way that not only brings peace but also brings deeper and greater understanding and enrichment to the marriage relationship. When we were engaged, we set up a few "traditions," or guidelines, to help us handle our conflicts.

For example, Bill and I hold hands when we discuss issues. (You are less likely to throw things if you are holding hands!) Some obvious traditions we include are: no violence, don't say anything we would be sorry for if it ended up being the last thing we had the opportunity to say to our mate, don't walk away unless one of us is feeling out of control (we communicate that, reschedule our discussion, and call for outside help if we can't solve the issue in a reasonable time frame).

Some of our friends used creative wording when they wrote their Conflict Covenant. Their contract with each other is "Rules for the Ring," and they use boxing terms. For example, the first four on their list are:

1. Hit the mat (pray).
2. No hitting below the belt (don't use words that are unkind or would tear down my mate).
3. Ring the bell (take a break if tempers get out of control).
4. Get a referee if the issue is getting ugly (go for counseling).

If you go to the home of our friends who have been happily married for over 40 years, you will find a big bowl of mini Snickers™ candy. In their Conflict Covenant they committed that if words get edgy and tempers rise, either of them can say, "Want to have a Snickers?" Eating a candy bar gives them time to calm down.

Below are some questions to help you create your own Conflict Covenant. Sit down with your spouse, talk through these issues, and create your own covenant. Be prepared to share some of your ideas with the other couples in your small group.

- What words will I use or not use?
- What actions with my body will I take or not take?
- What negative things did I see my parents, grandparents, or other couples do that I don't want us to do?
- What positive things have I observed in family or friends that I would like us to incorporate?
- When will we discuss issues?
- What will the kids be doing when we are discussing?
- What will we do if tempers or conversation escalate?
- How will we both know the issue is resolved?
- What will we do if we can't resolve the issue in a timely manner, and how long will we try to solve it on our own?

If you seek help, who will you go to first? second? Who will you not go to? Make sure you talk about the need to keep confidences. Pastors and professional marriage counselors are obligated to keep confidences. Lay leaders like Bible study leaders, friends, and family are not under such obligations, but they still can be trustworthy if they are people of good character who commit to keep your confidences. So talk about who you both feel comfortable talking with—preferably BEFORE you need to call for help!

Breaking Down the Walls

Unresolved issues can build like a wall, brick by brick, incident by incident, until there is a wall between the two of you. But God came to give us and our relationships a fresh start. It is called forgiveness.

We have tried to pattern forgiveness after Christ and His ultimate act of forgiveness on the cross. To give "forgiveness handles" that you can grasp in a practical way, we have come up with six statements that provide a working definition. We will show you God's plan of forgiveness and lead you through the story of Joseph to show how a real person chose to forgive.[5]

SIX STATEMENTS OF FORGIVENESS

1. I forgive _____ for _____.
     (name the person)   (name the offense)

"If we confess our sins, He is faithful and righteous to forgive us our sins and to cleanse us from all unrighteousness" (1 John 1:9).

Perhaps you are familiar with the story of Joseph. He's the guy with the coat of many colors, sold into slavery by his own family. He ended up in Egypt and was working as a servant to Pharaoh. Pharaoh's wife made a play for him and he ran away to protect his integrity. She lied and he was tossed into jail where a couple of people who said they'd help him didn't. He spent years in prison for a crime he didn't commit! If anyone had a right to be bitter, it was Joseph. Instead he chose the path God could bless: forgiveness. Joseph was blessed by God and God elevated him to second in command in the most powerful country of the day. Then one day his family showed up because there was a famine and they were hungry. What would you do?

Joseph could have done anything—he had the means, motive, and opportunity. In Genesis 45, God tells the story of how Joseph handled this difficult family situation. In verses 3-4 Joseph said to his brothers, "I am Joseph! Is my father still living?" But his brothers were too terrified to answer him.

Then Joseph said to his brothers, "Please, come near me," and they came near. "I am Joseph, your brother, the one you sold into Egypt." Here Joseph modeled an important step in the process of forgiveness. It is important to specifically name the offense. Vagueness in dealing with forgiveness only leads to doubts about whether forgiveness has truly been achieved.

The greatest example of forgiveness is the forgiveness Jesus Christ has offered us. He has granted each of us who trust Him freedom from guilt. This is indeed good news! But the good news starts with a very tough reality. "All have sinned and fall short of the glory of God" (Rom. 3:23).

Too often this step gets skipped. Maybe you think your hurt feelings are your problem. Maybe you are upset by what your spouse did, but you think he or she had the right to do whatever brings happiness. Maybe you are afraid to bring up pains from the past. Or maybe you don't know how. If you are looking for a clear path of freedom, be specific.

2. I admit that _____ was wrong.
          (name the offense)

"All have sinned and fall short of the glory of God" (Rom. 3:23).

This is God's way of saying we are all wrong— imperfect—and in need of forgiveness. Paul increased the seriousness of forgiveness in Romans 6:23 when he wrote, "The wages of sin is death." Paul understood forgiveness to be a life-and-death issue that begins with the honest confession of wrong. In our politically correct world, we often feel uncomfortable saying something is wrong. We may feel we are being critical or judgmental. If no wrong was done, however, there is nothing to forgive. And if the goal is forgiveness with the hope of restored intimacy, we aren't being a critic or a judge. We are taking fearless steps of love.

When Joseph's brother's approached him he said, "Don't be worried or angry with yourselves for selling me here, because God sent me ahead of you to preserve life" (Gen. 45:5). Why in the world did Joseph say, "Don't be worried or angry?" Because of what they did, they should have been worried and angry!

In verse 9 Joseph made a call to repentance. "Return quickly to my father and say to him, 'This is what your son Joseph says: "God has made me lord of all Egypt. Come down to me without delay"'" (Gen. 45:9).

Joseph understood there could be no real reconciliation without real repentance. If you are the offending party you need to own your issue, ask God to forgive you, then ask your mate to forgive you. If you are the one who was offended, you should forgive your spouse privately and pray God will convict him or her of the wrong choices made. Or you honestly confront—which works much better if you have already forgiven your spouse! If you forgive first, you are able to convey your concerns without the intense anger or emotion that sometimes clouds the issues.

3. I do not expect _____ to make up for what he or she has done.
           (name the person)

"If anyone is in Christ, there is a new creation; old things have passed away, and look,
new things have come" (2 Cor. 5:17).

This is a courageous statement of reality. Your spouse cannot make up for the mistakes that have been committed. The hurt of the action will continue to pain you and the memory of the irritation will linger. Nothing can undo what was done. Once an offense is committed, it cannot be uncommitted, so you need to let your spouse off the hook. Even an apology doesn't make up for it. Even restitution doesn't make up for it. If your spouse has hurt you, what you can do is forgive and give the opportunity for repentance. You can't make up for mistakes, but you can start over.

If you persist in waiting until your spouse makes up for the mistake, the pain of the mistake will control your life. Every time you are reminded of the event, the pain will shoot through your heart. Every time you try to trust, the pain will trip you up. The person you were once so much in love with will become unattractive in your eyes and consistently irritating in your heart.

You can't wait on living and loving until someone "makes up" for an offense. That's like pushing a permanent pause button on your own life and on key vital relationships—like your marriage. Joseph didn't push pause. Joseph knew his brothers couldn't go back and undo what they had done to him. He didn't wait to grow personally until they apologized. He would have been waiting a long time! Instead he decided to say, "Debt cancelled. You don't owe me." This freed him to see the issue from God's point of view and get a new take on it. This models what Jesus did on the cross:

> He erased the certificate of debt, with its obligations,
> that was against us and opposed to us, and has
> taken it out of the way by nailing it to the cross.
>
> Colossians 2:14

4. I will not use _____ to define who _____ is.
             (name the offense)   (name the person)

"Blessed be the God and Father of our Lord Jesus Christ, who has blessed us with every spiritual blessing in the heavens, in Christ; for He chose us in Him, before the foundation of the world, to be holy and blameless in His sight. In love He predestined us to be adopted through Jesus Christ for Himself, according to His favor and will, to the praise of His glorious grace that He favored us with in the Beloved. In Him we have redemption through His blood, the forgiveness of our trespasses, according to the riches of His grace that He lavished on us with all wisdom and understanding. He made known to us the mystery of His will, according to His good pleasure that He planned in Him for the administration of the days of fulfillment—to bring everything together in the Messiah, both things in heaven and things on earth in Him. In Him we were also made His inheritance, predestined according to the purpose of the One who works out everything in agreement with the decision of His will, so that we who had already put our hope in the Messiah might bring praise to His glory. In Him you also, when you heard the word of truth, the gospel of your salvation—in Him when you believed—were sealed with the promised Holy Spirit. He is the down payment of our inheritance, for the redemption of the possession, to the praise of His glory. This is why, since I heard about your faith in the Lord Jesus and your love for all the saints, I never stop giving thanks for you as I remember you in my prayers. [I pray] that the God of our Lord Jesus Christ, the glorious Father, would give you a spirit of wisdom and revelation in the knowledge of Him. [I pray] that the eyes of your heart may be enlightened so you may know what is the hope of His calling, what are the glorious riches of His inheritance among the saints, and what is the immeasurable greatness of His power to us who believe, according to the working of His vast strength" (Eph. 1:3-19).

When you define your spouse by the negative impact he or she has had on your life, you make that person bigger than life. You have given another person the ability to determine the state of your life.

When it comes to forgiving yourself for the things you have done, this step is vital. When you define yourself by the things you have done wrong you encourage a process of decay. If you think you deserve an unhealthy life, you will live out an unhealthy life. If you think you deserve to be punished, you will live out a self-destructive life. If you think you are a failure, you will avoid the path of success.

> Carefully read Ephesians 1:3-19 on page 68 and underline words
> and phrases that define who and what you really are if you have
> accepted Christ as your Savior.

If you define yourself as the object of God's grace and an adopted child who is in line for God's favor, you will pursue healthy avenues of growth and development.

When you define someone as the person who ruined your life or a monster or other labels of their wrongdoing, you make them the victimizer and you the victim. Who wants to go through life as the victim? Letting go of labels and name calling frees you to grow personally. The Bible says that "as he thinks within himself, so he is" (Prov. 23:7). If all you dwell on is the issue or the person who wronged you, it will keep you and the relationship stuck in the mud and mire of negativity. Forgiveness frees you both to move forward.

Joseph could have defined his brothers as traitors, scum, people who ruined his life. Instead he called them brothers. Free your mate and your marriage by dropping the name calling and negative labels.

5. I will not manipulate _____ with this offense.
                     (name the person)

"Do not repay anyone evil for evil. Try to do what is honorable in everyone's eyes. If possible, on your part, live at peace with everyone. Friends, do not avenge yourselves; instead, leave room for His wrath. For it is written: Vengeance belongs to Me; I will repay, says the Lord" (Rom. 12:17-19).

"If possible, on your part, live at peace." God is acknowledging that resolving interpersonal conflicts is a brave choice. There are two roads you can take: manipulation or making peace.

Manipulation is an attempt to emotionally blackmail another person. It is an attempt to protect yourself from the influence another person has on you. There is something in the human spirit that believes we can control another's influence through manipulation. Every act of manipulation confirms that the one who hurt you still has control of your life. Your approach to life shows you are still afraid of what this person might do to you. You try to get to others before they get to you. You run in an endless circle of self-protection, never enjoying the freedom of truly living.

Jesus does not constantly bring up our past sins to force us to do His will. Rather, He calls us to walk with Him as new creatures who have been set free from the past and from our mistakes. We are encouraged to live as saints rather than as recovering sinners. This does not mean God ignores the influence of our past. He has committed Himself to helping us grow through our past and reach a new life. We would be wise to look forward to the life ahead rather than constantly try to overcome the past.

Instead of manipulating, Joseph acted toward his brothers like a healthy brother would act, regardless of their actions. That is what will save a marriage: when you behave like a healthy partner, even if your spouse doesn't! Forgiveness isn't something you only do for others, you also do it for yourself and your relationship. Forgiveness protects your heart and your ability to create a healthy marriage even if you are the only one working on it. Notice the healthy choice Joseph made toward his family:

> You can settle in the land of Goshen and be near me—
> you, your children, and grandchildren, your sheep, cattle,
> and all you have. There I will sustain you, for there will be
> five more years of famine. Otherwise, you, your household,
> and everything you have will become destitute.
> Genesis 45:10-11

Making peace means giving up your right to manipulate someone based upon past offenses. Making peace means acting toward them like a healthy person would act, regardless of how they act toward you. Making peace is taking the high road, not stooping to the offenders level to offend or get back at him or her. Making peace will bring you peace. Choose the path toward peace by refusing to manipulate.

6. I will not allow _____ to stop my personal growth.
                  (name the offense)

"Grow in the grace and knowledge of our Lord and Savior Jesus Christ.
To Him be the glory both now and to the day of eternity" (2 Pet. 3:18).

This step is probably the most important. The banner cry of the Bible is growth!

Read 2 Corinthians 10:15; Ephesians 4:11-15; Philippians 1:9-10; and 2 Peter 3:18 below.

"Our hope is that, as your faith continues to grow, our area of activity among you will greatly expand" (2 Cor. 10:15, NIV).

"He personally gave some to be apostles, some prophets, some evangelists, some pastors and teachers, for the training of the saints in the work of ministry, to build up the body of Christ, until we all reach unity in the faith and in the knowledge of God's Son, [growing] into a mature man with a stature measured by Christ's fullness. Then we will no longer be little children, tossed by the waves and blown around by every wind of teaching, by human cunning with cleverness in the techniques of deceit. But speaking the truth in love, let us grow in every way into Him who is the head—Christ" (Eph. 4:11-15).

"I pray this: that your love will keep on growing in knowledge and every kind of discernment, so that you can determine what really matters and can be pure and blameless in the day of Christ" (Phil. 1:9-10).

"Grow in the grace and knowledge of our Lord and Savior Jesus Christ" (2 Pet. 3:18).

Based on these Scriptures, answer the following questions.

In what areas does God desire growth in your life?

_____

_____

Why does He want you to grow?

_____

_____

What is the ultimate goal of your growth?

_____

_____

Too often we allow the sinful offenses of others to dictate the course of our lives. It is almost as though we think we are punishing the ones who hurt us by refusing to pull our lives together. Or we are emotionally committed to keeping things in our families the way they have historically been. If our ancestors were bitter, we are bitter. If our ancestors were prone to depression, we are prone to depression. This applies to everything from alcoholism and anger to lack of confidence.

"It was not you who sent me here, but God. He has made me a father to Pharaoh, lord of his entire household, and ruler over all the land of Egypt" (Gen. 45:8). Notice Joseph's elevated leadership position. That kind of responsibility isn't given to an immature individual. Joseph climbed the success ladder in life because he chose to forgive over and over again.

We don't forgive because people deserve forgiveness or have earned it. None of us deserve forgiveness, but God in His mercy and grace extended forgiveness to redeem the relationship with us. We forgive, not because someone does or doesn't deserve forgiveness; we forgive to redeem or to restore the relationship. Forgiveness protects our own integrity and the ability to have whole, healthy relationships with people. If we hold bitterness against one person, it seeps out like toxic waste and negatively impacts all relationships. If we forgive, it spreads hope, joy, and love into all our relationships. Forgiveness is like a people magnet. People like being around those who are like Jesus: merciful, gracious, and forgiving.

Forgiveness is a protection for our marriage relationship. It gives us the ability to stay in love for a lifetime. If you each selfishly hold on to your right to be angry, you will keep your anger and bitterness—but lose each other! Forgiveness sets you both free to love.

Forgiveness gives us the ability to stay in love for a lifetime.

Don't be surprised by the conflict in your relationship. If you had no needs and your attitude was always unselfish, you could have constant peace between you and your spouse. But because yours is a relationship between people, you should expect the waffles and spaghetti to compete for room at the table. We are different because of gender, personality, past experiences, or just the fact we are all imperfect and human. We will hurt one another. Master forgiveness and you will be free to experience God's best in marriage, family, and community. Forgiveness is the key that unlocks the potential of all relationships.

Reread Colossians 3:12-13 (p. 60).

What is the standard for how you are to forgive others?

_____

_____

How did Christ forgive you?

_____

_____

Spend time praying with your spouse. Ask God to make you a forgiving family who spreads hope, joy, and love in your world.

1. Daniel J. Canary and Tara M. Emmers-Sommer with Sandra Faulkner, Sex and Gender Differences in Personal Relationships (New York: Guilford Press, 1997), 82
2. Ibid.
3. Ibid.
4. Ibid, 31.
5. This is a brief overview. For more details on the process of forgiveness and reconciliation, see Bill and Pam Farrel, Love, Honor and Forgive (Downers Grove, IL: InterVarsity Press, 2000).

SPAGHETTI "Who is a God like You, removing iniquity and passing over rebellion" (Mic. 7:18).

Describe the last time you really got mad at your husband.

_____

_____

_____

_____

How might this instance have been related to his "waffleness"?

_____

_____

_____

How might you have been particularly "noodly" in this instance?

_____

_____

_____

Read Micah 7:18-20 in your Bible. How can you demonstrate Christlikeness in how you handle conflict with your husband?

_____

_____

_____

"Who is a God like You, removing iniquity and passing over rebellion" (Mic. 7:18).   # WAFFLE

Describe the last time you really got mad at your wife.

_____

_____

_____

_____

How might this instance have been related to her "spaghetti-like" state?

_____

_____

_____

How might your "waffleness" have contributed to this conflict?

_____

_____

_____

Read Micah 7:18-20 in your Bible. How can you demonstrate Christlikeness in how you handle conflict with your wife?

_____

_____

_____

week five
Functioning as a Family

Serve one another through love.

Galatians 5:12

Viewer Guide

Everything in your home will go better if you raise the motivation level.

•maximize gender

•pay attention to personalities

   Lion   Beaver   Otter   Retriever

What motivates:

Lions _____

Otters _____

Retrievers _____

Beavers _____

These four personality types are the combination of two traits:

1. Extrovert _____

   Introvert _____

2. Task-oriented _____

   People-oriented _____

Waffles and Spaghetti at Home

A woman marries a man expecting he will change, but he doesn't. A man marries a woman expecting she won't change and she does. Despite the frustration between men and women, they still desire to live together. People long for the stability of companionship, the security of emotional acceptance, and the passion of sexual desire. A man and woman enter into marriage with the expectation that joy and happiness will follow. Then life gets in the way. Bills need to be paid, chores demand our attention, cars need to be maintained, and finances must be managed.

How does a couple go about dividing the responsibilities of life? What chores does the husband oversee? What tasks should the wife be in charge of? What responsibilities should be handled together? Are there chores best handled by women? by men? These questions have plagued couples throughout history as each generation wrestles with answers that fit the culture of the day.

Historically, women's work has centered around the home. It has been assumed that women are more domestic and have a natural desire to develop a nurturing environment in their homes. Men, on the other hand, have been relegated to yard work, analytical pursuits, and maintenance of the family machinery. It has been assumed that they handle these areas best because they can conquer them.

There is no Jew or Greek, slave or free,

male or female; for you are all one in Christ Jesus.

Galatians 3:28

Do gender stereotypes factor into your decisions regarding
who does what around your house? ☒ yes ☒ no

Does the mention of the division of household tasks cause
feelings of anxiety and resentment to build up within you?
☒ yes ☒ no

Before you go any further, please stop and pray. Submit to God any negative feelings you have about the roles of husband and wife at home. Ask God to give you a teachable spirit and a willingness to change your attitudes and actions toward tasks that must be accomplished in your home.

We (Bill and Pam) believe in delegating based on strengths, spiritual giftedness, and level of interest rather than society's stereotypes. If Dad is the better cook, let him cook. If Mom loves to paint, let her stand on the ladder. The key is that the person to whom the task is delegated should also have the authority to do things his or her way, in his or her timing. If we aren't willing to pitch in on a task, we should not comment or criticize. The job of the spouse who is not responsible for the delegated task is to be grateful!

Read Colossians 3:15.

"Let the peace of the Messiah, to which you were also called in one body, control your hearts. Be thankful" (Col. 3:15).

When it comes to your spouse's performance of household tasks, have you been more:

☒ critical? ☒ grateful? ☒ insistent?

How can thanking your spouse for taking on household tasks (even ones he or she is "supposed" to do) bring peace to this touchy area of who does what?

_____

_____

_____

How will you thank your spouse today for a way he or she serves

your family? _____

_____

ONE AT A TIME

Because men tend to process life in individual boxes, the average man prefers tasks that can be done one at a time. He wants to do the first task until it is done and then move on to the next. If it is a creative task, he may even stay in the box and admire his work for awhile. Because he loves his wife and feels great about himself when she is proud of him, he usually wants her to join him in admiring his expert craftsmanship. The nature of the task is not as important as the opportunity to focus on one task at a time.

FIND A BALANCE

Because women have the ability to connect everything in life, the average woman can manage several tasks at a time better than the average man. Finding a balance in the operation of the home is a nonnegotiable necessity for her. The tasks she considers vital must be addressed with a workable plan or everything in the home will feel out of place. It doesn't necessarily matter to her if she attends to these tasks or if others in the family get them done as long as they are accomplished. The actual tasks are not as important as the balance.

WORK THE SYSTEM

As you look at your family system, you will discover many tasks in your home are best done in conjunction with others. These will most likely be preferred by the wife. Some of the tasks, however, are best accomplished as individual tasks and will typically be better handled by the husband. In our home I (Bill) oversee all the car maintenance, which is a predictably male activity. It surprises some to learn that I usually do the laundry also. As Pam and I analyzed the way we work as a couple, we recognized that Pam's creativity can get in the way of mundane tasks like laundry. She will get the laundry sorted and put the first load in, but her creative juices start to flow and she becomes involved in other tasks. Once she is in high gear it is quite possible she will not get back to the laundry. I prefer to focus on one task at a time. When I am doing the laundry, I am doing the laundry. I may fiddle with other activities, but they are only diversions to keep me busy while I am waiting for the next step in the main task of getting our clothes clean.

WHAT IT TAKES

Find out what is really important to your spouse. Arguments and misunderstandings develop because we assume we know what is important to our spouse. You don't want to guess; you want to know what is important!

> Write the life activities listed on the top of the next page on index cards.
> You and your spouse will each need a set. Rank each item 1, 2, or 3.
> 1 = It is very important to you. You would keep these activities even
>   if you never get to a 2 or 3 activity.
> 2 = It is important though not a main focus, but you don't feel it
>   can go undone.
> 3 = If it gets done, fine; if it doesn't, no sweat. These activities can
>   drop out of life when things get hectic or the quality can suffer
>   a bit and it won't make you crazy.

being in good physical shape

having a neat, clean home

having the family finances in order

maintaining correspondence

having quality intimacy/romance

having time with my children

having fun as a family

succeeding in my career

having a personal ministry/being involved in church

participating in extracurricular activities (community involvement,
    career enhancement, philanthropic activities)

having a nice car(s)

furthering my education

achieving more financial success

having time alone

spending time with God

spending time with my mate (talking, relating nonsexually)

having time for a hobby

other: _____

Compare your cards. Which things are ranked the same? Mark those
with a star. You're less likely to argue over those areas. Circle the
areas that have the greatest differences. You'll have to negotiate in
those areas. They are hot spots.

Next prioritize the cards. Maybe you both indicated that a neat, clean house was
important. Clean means different things to different people. Bill and I found out early
in our marriage that the bedroom and the living room need to be neat for me to be
happy. Bill has to have a clean kitchen with the dishes done and put away or he can't
relax. We should take responsibility for that which is a high priority to us!

Another area of possible conflict will be those areas you both marked as 3 but in
reality are 1 in daily life. For example, neither Bill nor I love to work with the finances,
but the bills have to be paid! Because Bill was a math major and he's great at it, he's
taken on the task. But I have pity on his sacrifice, so I usually bake him cookies and
sit down to sort the bills or write the checks or file—something to keep him company.

Read Galatians 5:13 again (p. 76).

What should be the key action and attitude in your marriage?

_____

Imagine your spouse has just asked you to complete some household responsibility. Identify whether the responses listed below indicate resentment, selfishness, or service.

That's your job. _____

I shouldn't even have to ask you to help. _____

How else can I help? _____

Happy to do it. _____

I'll get to it eventually. _____

I will, but I'm not happy about it. _____

Look at those statements again. Do you most often exhibit resentment, selfishness, or service to your mate? Pray about your response.

SOLD TO THE HIGHEST BIDDER

When I was a little girl, I played a game called "Pit." It is a mock version of the trading that happens on Wall Street. In "Pit," players try to gather all of one commodity. They trade other players for the commodity they prize most. One player might trade four wheat just to get two corns. That is exactly what you'll need to do when you come to the negotiating table with your spouse. If something is really important to you, you'll have to compensate in other areas.

"I'll trade you childcare on Mondays and Thursdays if you'll do this stack of errands. I hate errands!" Bill exclaimed.

"That's fair. And since I'll be running back and forth, I'll pick up the boys from school. That way you can have some uninterrupted time to work on the house, yard, paperwork, and bills," I responded.

"That's workable. Who's going to take this stack of responsibilities?" he asked as he picked up the level 3 cards that neither of us wanted.

"Let's see. What's in it?"

"Let's divide and conquer the laundry. You sort it on Monday. I'll wash and fold it the next few days. Thursday you can oversee the boys as they put it away. Fair?"

"Fair. How about lunches?"

"The boys can make their own. They can each take responsibility for keeping a car clean this year, too."

"Good idea. I'll take homework and any errands that come with that," I volunteered.

"Great. But I'll set aside one day close to science fair time to help," said Bill.

"Of course. That's tradition now. How about this stack of ministry priorities?"

"Let's take that on our getaway and pray over them. We need to decide which to do now, which to have our new staff person do, and which are great ideas for the future. Pam, you can easily fill your days with good things and not get to your writing. God has called you to that, and I want to help you set some boundaries so you can write."

I looked at my pile of 1s. Romance for Bill and me, the boys' activities, writing, women's ministry, exercise. It would be tough to get all those things accomplished if I didn't set some boundaries and protect my time. I remembered the year Bill fought to get my attention. He missed me and wanted more time with me. That's how the cards all started. Bill and I both wanted more time together, and we were having a tough time finding it.

DON'T TALK ABOUT IT, BE ABOUT IT!

There are only 24 hours in a day, and as a team you have to come up with a workable plan on how to spend those hours. Rather than try to change one another, the wise couple will utilize their differences to maximize the effectiveness of the family. The important issue is not who does what task, it's the attitude with which you do it.

> The important issue is not who does what task,
> it's the attitude with which you do it.

Read the following verses. Record attitudes that can motivate you to serve your family, even when you don't feel like it.

Mark 9:35 _____

Galatians 1:10 _____

Ephesians 6:7 _____

Choose a phrase from one of the verses you just read that you can repeat to yourself when you feel anger or resentment coming. For example, one of my (Pam's) favorite is "Who am I trying to please?" My goal is to please God.

Waffles and Spaghetti as Parents

Mom is usually the primary caregiver when the kids are young. One of the reasons is the ability of mom to nurse her newborn child, ensuring a close, constant emotional bond. As kids grow, Dad gets increasingly involved as he becomes more comfortable with their needs and feels more competent to meet those needs. When kids enter late adolescence, they tend to look to their dads for help in making major life decisions.

THE POWER OF A WAFFLE

It can be discouraging to Mom that the kids turn to Dad for the major decisions when she has been there for all their ups and downs, broken bones and broken hearts, and a thousand other experiences. The importance of Mom is indisputable, but Dad has an influence on his kids that Mom cannot duplicate. We have noticed that kids whose dads have been actively involved and aggressively interested in their lives are more confident and more likely to make healthy decisions. Conversely, teens whose dads were absent or uninvolved are more insecure and make decisions that complicate their lives. In terms of future success, the discernment to recognize a good choice in a mate, and the ability to maintain emotional balance in life, Dad is the difference!

While children do tend to turn to Mom for comfort and reassurance, Dad's role is just as vital. A child's relationship with Dad is the most important factor in determining how he or she will react to the rest of the world. For example, "an experiment carried out on six-month-old boys found that those who had most contact with their fathers were least disturbed when a stranger of either sex picked them up. Similarly, a recent American study shows that the less frequently babies of both sexes are dressed and bathed by their fathers, the longer they cry when they are left alone with an adult they don't know."[1]

In addition to making children more confident socially, fathers make a significant contribution to their intellectual development. "The rocking, talking and touching that fathers provide in response to their children's signals teaches a baby that it can affect other people by its actions, and encourages its intellectual curiosity. As a result, research shows that the more contact a child has with its father, the more advanced it is likely to be. This effect is more marked for boys, though other aspects of a father's behavior can also have a direct effect on a daughter's intellectual development."[2]

THE INFLUENCE OF A GOOD SPAGHETTI DINNER

Mom plays a powerful role in the life of a child. Because she integrates life and emotionally connects to those closest to her, Mom provides the first primary trust relationship with a child. The more bonded a child is to Mom the first few weeks and months of life, the stronger his or her ability to trust others is.

Dr. Jack Raskin, child psychiatrist at Children's Orthopedic Hospital and at the University of Washington, states, "No psychological event is as important as the bonding that occurs between the mother and child in the first moments of the child's life."[3] Psychoanalyst John Bowlby points out that this attachment to Mom is the "foundation stone of ... personality." Bowlby explains that the mother-child attachment is evident throughout childhood and only weakens as the teen years progress because more adults become important to the child.[4] In Unfinished Business, Maggie Scarf says that when this basic relationship is disturbed and the mother is absent, especially during the first four to five years of life, "the child experiences acute psychological pain. This anguish has three distinct stages: protest, despair, and, finally, detachment. When the child reaches this last stage ... he no longer cares. And if this separation from mother is too long, the process may never be reversed. Some children literally die from the absence of this protective and absorbing emotional bond."[5]

LIFESTYLE ADJUSTMENTS

Both Mom and Dad have to adjust to the change of lifestyle that accompanies the birth of a baby. Dad needs to create a new box that provides time for his kids and interest in being their dad. With the birth of each child, Mom's emotional capacity increases and her life gets fuller. She may assume her husband has likewise expanded his emotional horizons. But he has simply added a box to the husband box. He still wants the husband box to get the same attention, and he still wants to go to easy boxes to de-stress. Mom can help if she chooses not to get her feelings hurt if Dad feels the need for a game of racquetball or a round of golf to get his equilibrium again.

The transition to parenthood is packed with responsibility. Transitions in life can seem overwhelming, parenthood especially, but transitions are normal. When you look back on these events, they will be some of your strongest memories.

What transitions is your family experiencing right now?

_____

How do you think you're handling these transitions?

_____

"I the LORD do not change" (Mal. 3:6, NIV).

How can Malachi 3:6 comfort and stabilize you through all life's

transitions? _____

E X T R O V E R T

People Oriented

PERSONALITY TYPE ONE
Popular; Sanguine
Brawner: Otter; Phillips: Expressive
DISC: Inspirational; Littauer: Yellow like the sun
Biblical Example: John the Baptist

CHARACTERISTICS: creative, spontaneous, excellent people skills

PRIMARY WEAKNESSES: lack of perseverance; because they love a party they can seem shallow and flippant to some

MOTIVATED BY: attention (the more public the better)

WHEN THEY GROW UP THEY WANT TO BE: actors, comedians, stars in soap operas, cheerleaders, salesmen, Cinderella, Miss Piggy

I N T R O V E R T

PERSONALITY TYPE THREE
Peaceful; Phlegmatic

Brawner: Retriever; Phillips: Amiable
DISC: Steady; Littauer: Green like grass
Biblical Example: Barnabas

CHARACTERISTICS: peaceful, supportive, loyal, don't like to be defined by their performance

PRIMARY WEAKNESSES: slow to make decisions and take actions

MOTIVATED BY: respect and acceptance

WHEN THEY GROW UP THEY WANT TO BE: golf pros, rich so they don't have to work, live on lakes with boats and canoes, take long vacations, have more recess

Task Oriented

PERSONALITY TYPE TWO
Powerful, Choleric
Brawner: Lion; Phillips: Driver
DISC: Dominant; Littauer: Red like fire
Biblical Example: Peter

CHARACTERISTICS: decision makers, natural leaders

PRIMARY WEAKNESSES: lack of empathy; bull-dozer mentality

MOTIVATED BY: power and choices

WHEN THEY GROW UP THEY WANT TO BE: kings and queens,
the president, owners of big houses and limousines, highway patrolmen,
football players

PERSONALITY TYPE FOUR
Perfect, Melancholy
Brawner: Beaver; Phillips: Analytical
DISC: Cautious; Littauer: Blue like the ocean
Biblical Example: Martha

CHARACTERISTICS: creative, want things done right, patient, detailed,
always thinking and processing, evidence collectors

PRIMARY WEAKNESSES: can be negative and depressed because of
a glass half empty outlook; can be obsessive

MOTIVATED BY: answers and structure

WHEN THEY GROW UP THEY WANT TO BE: musicians, artists, poets,
bankers, Mozart, Garfield

MOTIVATE ME!

Boys are like waffles, girls are like pasta. There are definite gender differences, but layered atop these are distinct, God-given personality traits. There are many quality personality assessment tools available that can help you better understand the personalities of your children.

We have combined some of that information to create the chart on pages 86-87.[6] This chart contains four quadrants, each with a unique personality. The personality types on the left-hand page (p. 86) are primarily people-driven personalities. People are this child's priority.

Our son Zach has this trait. If he has a choice between breaking down the set after church or baby-sitting the staff kids, he'll entertain the kids in a heartbeat. He had to create a homework club so he could get his homework done. He studies best over conversation and chips. Our son Brock, on the other hand, would rather lock himself in his room to study because he says, "Studying in a group is a waste of time. You have to wait until everyone gets it and half the time they aren't even talking about anything remotely related!"

Brock is task-oriented. The task-oriented personalities are the two on the right-hand page (p. 87). It isn't that task-oriented people don't like socializing; they do. But if they have to choose between getting the job done and talking, they'll get the job done every time. If I want something done at home, I'll ask Brock and he'll have it done in an instant so he can go on to the tasks he enjoys most. Many people that are great with technology have this personality trait. Brock can do almost anything on the computer. He can fix VCRs and set up sound systems. He can build a set of bookshelves or a desk without even looking at the directions. He loves math. Life to Brock is one big equation. You put in the right variables, and you'll get the desired outcome every time.

But if you want counseling, don't ask Brock. His answer will always be the same. "You are having a problem with temptation. Just don't do it anymore. Problem solved." If a person wants sympathy, Zach is a much better counselor. He'll sit down with a person, usually because he can read discouragement or depression in a person's face. He'll ask, "What's wrong?" He'll listen attentively, he'll pray, and he'll carry the other person's pain with him.

INTROVERTS AND EXTROVERTS

Those personality types above the center line are extroverts. Those below the line are introverts. This doesn't necessarily mean one is loud and the other quiet. Extroverts process life from the outside in while introverts process life from the inside out. As a result, extroverts feel more secure and at peace when all the ducks of their lives are lined up. They tend to ask questions like: Am I spending enough time with God?

Am I balanced in my personal disciplines of prayer, Bible study, witnessing, fasting, and memorization? Am I spending enough time with my family? Am I spending enough time with my friends? Is my work helping me reach the goals I have set for myself? They are life organizers, and if they feel they have the right organizational plan they are as happy as clams.

Introverts ask questions like: Do I feel connected to God? Is my personal prayer life deep? Am I sensitive to God's call and leading? Am I connected with those I love? Am I relating well to my friends? Is my work fulfilling? Do I have a sense of personal peace and tranquility? When these people are emotionally connected and fulfilled, they are at peace.

There are quiet extroverts. Zach is an extrovert. For years we couldn't figure out how someone who doesn't seem to talk could have so many friends! Our son Caleb is a confident and friendly introvert. Caleb is miserable if he is not emotionally connected to those he cares about.

Write your children's names in the chart next to the personality type you think best describes them. Compare your answers with those of your spouse.

Read Proverbs 22:6:

"Teach a youth about the way he should go; even when he is old he will not depart from it" (Prov. 22:6).

"Way he should go" means according to the child's God-given bent. Based on that understanding, why is it important for you to understand and appreciate your child's personality type and passions?

_____

_____

HINTS FOR RAISING A WAFFLE

Because women are much more verbal than men and because women can tap into their emotions easier than most men, one of the biggest favors you can do for a son is to raise his vocabulary, especially when it comes to expressing his emotions.

Remember that men are more likely to open up if you go into their favorite box. Sons are the same. If you want him to open up emotionally and share more details, go into one of his favorite boxes (favorite sport, favorite place to eat, favorite hobby) and then listen and repeat key phrases or ask specific questions.

One thing that seems to get a son talking is to feed him. Studies say that a man gets happier when fed. Give him a favorite snack and ask questions.

HINTS FOR UNDERSTANDING YOUR NOODLING DAUGHTER

The best thing you can do for your daughter is patiently listen to her and touch her often. Because we have not raised a daughter, we can only talk with you about what we have seen in the lives of young ladies who have been part of our ministry over the past two decades. What is obvious from our experience is that girls need to talk through their lives. They process life verbally. They learn about being good friends by talking with their parents. They discover how to respond to hurts and disappointments by talking through their experiences with their parents. They learn to guide their emotions in life by talking them through with their parents. If their parents are not available, girls don't stop talking. They turn to peers or other trusted adults. Other adult attention is not as effective because the emotional bond is not the same they have with Mom and Dad. The interest of peers is not as effective because they are not mature enough to give healthy insight.

The other interesting corollary to listening is the importance of physical touch with daughters. Kind, encouraging, appropriate touching releases endorphins in the body. Endorphins are chemicals that make people "feel" better. It is as if they are one of God's rewards for doing the right thing. When a daughter has loving, respectful physical contact with her parents, she feels better about whatever she is doing. By demonstrating consistent affection, parents help their daughters associate good feelings with the activities of life. When endorphins are released during conversation, daughters associate conversation with feeling good. When making decisions is accompanied by reassuring touches, she associates decision-making with feeling good. When conflict is worked through and concluded with physical affection, even conflict resolution will be associated with feeling good. Because your daughter will relate all that happens in her life to the emotional state she was in at the time, you do her a great favor when you make physical affection a consistent part of her life.

Read Hebrews 12:5-11 in your Bible. What is one of the greatest favors you can do your sons and daughters?

_____

Why is that a favor? _____

_____

"The child should spend a substantial amount of time with somebody who's crazy about him [or her]."[8]

"Sons are indeed a heritage from the Lord, children a reward. …
Happy is the man who has filled his quiver with them" (Ps. 127:3,5).

Dad: How can you let your kids know you feel rewarded and

happy to be their dad? _____

_____

_____

"Let your father and mother have joy, and let her who gave birth
to you rejoice" (Prov. 23:25).

Mom: How can you let your kids know you rejoice that they

were born? _____

_____

_____

1. John Nicholson, Men and Women (Oxford, England: Oxford University Press, 1984), 131, quoted in Bill and Pam Farrel, Men Are Like Waffles—Women Are Like Spaghetti (Eugene, OR: Harvest House, 2001), 168-69.
2. Ibid.
3. Brenda Hunter, Where Have All the Mothers Gone? (Grand Rapids: Zondervan, 1982), 88.
4. Ibid.
5. Ibid., 89.
6. Adapted from Bill and Pam Farrel, 10 Best Decisions a Parent Can Make (Eugene, OR: Harvest House, 2006). Information about "when they grow up" is from Florence Littauer, Raising Christians—Not Just Children (Word: Dallas, TX, 1988), 73.
7. For more on personalities: Florence Littauer, Marita Littauer, Getting Along with Almost Anybody: The Complete Personality Book (Grand Rapids7: Fleming H. Revell, 1998); Jim and Suzette Brawner, Taming the Family Zoo: Maximizing Harmony and Minimizing Family Stress (Colorado Springs: NavPress, 1998); and Bob Phillips, The Delicate Art of Dancing with Porcupines: Learning to Appreciate the Finer Points of Others (Ventura, CA: Regal Books, 1989); for information on personality assessments visit John Trent's Web site www.ministryinsights.com; or for information on the DISC profile visit www.discinsights.com.
8. Hunter, 93.

SPAGHETTI

"Can a mother forget the baby at her breast and have no compassion on the child she has borne?" (Is. 49:15, NIV).

On a separate sheet of paper identify how you can be to your children a:

1. mentor (teach them necessary skills)

2. listener and communicator

3. consistent disciplinarian

4. parenting partner with your husband

5. spiritual guide

Discuss your responses with your husband. Are you willing to give up some control in order to let him parent the children as well? Accept and appreciate his "waffle" approach to child-rearing instead of expecting him to behave like a noodle.

On that same sheet of paper, write two or three things you admire about your husband as a father. Tell him!

If you don't have children (or even if you do), compliment your husband on the way he makes your house a home.

"Fathers, don't stir up anger in your children, but bring them up in the training and instruction of the Lord" (Eph. 6:1).

WAFFLE

On a separate sheet of paper identify how you can be to your children a:

1. mentor (teach them what you love)

2. listener and communicator

3. marshal (hold them accountable to reasonable expectations)

4. parenting partner with your wife

5. spiritual guide

Discuss your responses with your wife. Discover what she'd like you to do with your children. Honestly tell her if some of her expectations don't fit your "waffle box" personality, but be willing to make sacrifices to be the father they need.

On that same sheet of paper, write two or three things you admire about your wife as a mother. Tell her!

If you don't have children (or even if you do), compliment your wife on the way she makes your house a home.

week six
SucceedingTogether

Be devoted to one another in brotherly love.
Honor one another above yourselves.

Romans 12:10, NIV

Viewer Guide

In this session you will hear Bill Farrel say, "I realized I can help create the kind of wife I have."

You also can help create the kind of spouse you have. As you listen to the Farrels share a defining moment in their relationship, think of ways you can be a mirror to your spouse. Use this page to list your thoughts and ideas.

_____

_____

_____

_____

_____

_____

_____

_____

_____

_____

_____

_____

For the lyrics to "I Will Be Your Mirror," see page 112.

Waffles and Spaghetti Achieving Together

Both genders love to achieve. The interaction between men and women has not been called the "battle of the sexes" for nothing. We are all competitive, ambitious, and stubborn to some degree. It is not fair to say men love to produce while women love to nurture. Both genders love to produce, and we should see ourselves as intelligent, creative people.

Both men and women feel better about themselves when they have mastered a new concept or found an effective avenue for achieving goals. It is one of the great areas of life that men and women have in common. That is why husbands and wives talk about "building a life together." A family is not built just because you give birth to kids. It is built because you pursue financial, social, developmental, and cultural goals together.

> "The one who pursues righteousness and faithful love will find life, righteousness, and honor" (Prov. 21:21).

> "Seek first the kingdom of God and His righteousness, and all these things will be provided for you" (Matt. 6:33).

> Based on Proverbs 21:21 and Matthew 6:33, how will the wise husband and wife pursue their goals?

_____

In this pursuit, careers must be decided. Every couple wants to succeed in their choices of careers and find the balance that works best for their family. However, too often the assumption is made that men and women work the same. Husbands assume their wives would be happier if they could find work they liked. Wives often muse over how their husbands can seemingly leave their home life at home and their work life at work and never mix the two.

> As you read the following general differences between men and women, mark a star by the ones you personally know to be true.

Men like to take more risks than women. Generally, men are more willing to take risks and gain a greater level of satisfaction from the risk than their female counterparts. This is not to say women are afraid of risk or are unwilling to take risks in their career pursuits. Men just enjoy it more. One study entitled "The Testosterone Rush: A Study of Senior Marketing Executives" found that "men 'shot more from the hip,' while women carefully considered the alternatives before choosing a course of action. When it comes to decision-making, men were perceived to be faster on the draw … and were more apt to take risks. … Men also 'pay too much attention to the competition,' and are more short-term oriented."[1]

Women like consensus more than men. Life for the average female is a web of inter-connected relationships and issues. Relationships and decisions are interconnected. This does not mean she has to get along with everybody in the office. It simply means she will consider the broad impact of her decisions, and she will want the decision to benefit as many of the important people in her life as possible. "Women … build more consensus during decision-making … and acted more thoughtfully when choosing their course of action."[2] It is interesting to note that "men work longer hours" than women but they "perceive significantly lower coworker support compared to women," and "women are substantially more likely than men to report that they can talk to their coworkers and are close to and appreciated by their coworkers."[3]

As much as we like to think we all face challenges the same way and we all follow the same leadership styles, research does not support this. Men and women tend to lead differently. Men typically emphasize the achievement of orga-nizational goals as the highest priority of the work environment while women typically emphasize people and relationships.

Men and women learn differently. One of the reasons men and women approach the workplace differently is that they learn differently. We are able to learn the same information, but we process it differently. "Men, for example, tend to think more in terms of principles, while women think more in terms of relationships. Men gener-ally learn on a less personal level, while women tie thoughts to emotions." This is why "on achievement tests, men score higher on math and spatial concepts, while women outscore men in areas of language."[4]

Men and women cope with work stress differently. When men are faced with stress at work, they either focus on the task and get it done, or they divert attention to an activity that is easier for them. In school, male students will distract them-selves by watching more television than their female counterparts. It is almost comical to walk through the student union of any university and see the young men watching TV while the young women are in huddles talking. Women seek out conversation with others to cope with pressures. When they can talk through the process of their expectations, they can find handles for facing the stress. A woman will talk with parents, friends, trusted coworkers, or her husband, but the stress remains until she can talk it out.[5]

Women feel they have to work harder than men. In high school "women spent more hours in studying … and less hours in watching TV … This may be due to the fact that women … tend to attribute their achievement outcomes to effort while men attribute these to ability."[6]

Once a woman enters the workforce, she quickly realizes she has entered a male-dominated domain. "Despite a gradual increase in the number of women in managerial roles, they are still estimated to fill only 25% of managerial positions in Germany, 28% in Switzerland, 33% in the UK and 43% in Australia. ... At higher levels women are even more poorly represented, filling only 10% of senior level manage-ment positions in the United States."[7]

Women are affected more by their home life than men. This is one of the most obvi-ous arenas where the differences between men and women come into play. Because men see their lives in individual boxes, they approach work as its own pursuit. It is not attached to family life, it is not attached to friendships, and it is not attached to the emotional climate of their relationships. When a man goes to work, he goes to work.

Because women connect everything in life, work is an integrated pursuit. Her day at work affects her relationships at home and her relationships at home affect her work. She would like to separate the two but finds it is more work to keep them separate than to let them relate to one another. As a result, she enjoys her work more when her life at home is going well, and she enjoys her family more when her work is going well.

Parenthood impacts men and women differently. When women have children their world expands. Each child gains a place in her heart, and there seems to be no end to the number of children she can love and care for. Men are not so fortu-nate. Each child adds a new box to Dad's waffle, but kids are not boxes that men can ignore. They demand attention and are incessant about having Dad involved in their favorite activities. It is an incredible compliment that every kid wants his or her dad involved, but this involvement complicates his life. His career requires significant focus, and he knows each child should get the same intensity of focus from him. He gets frustrated because he can't keep that many boxes open at once. He must open them one at a time. When he has a family it is hard to find time to responsibly relax. A wise wife will help her husband find time to recharge.

With all these differences, how is a couple supposed to figure out God's will for their combined life and family?

Read Ephesians 6:6-9 in your Bible and fill in the blanks. Regardless of our differences, the Bible commands us all to work:

to accomplish _____

with a good _____

for _____ and not _____

with the knowledge you will receive a _____

Encourage Each Other's Dreams

The Apostle Paul explained this concept in Ephesians 5:28-29: "Husbands should love their wives as their own bodies … no one ever hates his own flesh, but provides and cares for it." A husband does himself a favor when he loves his wife by building into her personal growth. A wife will want to give back and encourage her husband when she is validated as a growing child of God. Bill believed in me as a writer long before I won any awards or published anything of significance. Bill looked at me through God's eyes and responded accordingly.

HOW A WAFFLE CAN ENCOURAGE HIS SPAGHETTI

It's not always easy being teammates. Pam and I had a several-month-long disagreement over her desire to spread her wings. She wanted to return to school and begin work on her writing career. We had a plan and she wanted to jump ahead of schedule. I didn't like it! We still had children at home full-time. Her desire to chase her goals put pressure on me to help with domestic duties beyond what I thought should be expected. Pam's dreams were an inconvenience to my life! I got angry with her! I fought for months before I came to my senses and realized I wasn't fighting Pam. I was fighting God. God had placed this dream in Pam and I was blocking it. Pam wasn't trying to make my life miserable—I was choosing that for myself.

I finally came to the point where I could encourage Pam in her pursuits, and I wanted to find a way to make up for the grief I had given her. One day I had to be on the campus where Pam attended class. Before Pam left for school that morning she said, "Think of me when you are on campus today." That's when I got an idea that was as big as the resistance I had thrown her way.

She was in a medieval literature class that morning. The professor had just announced that romance was dead. He pointed out that it was an idealistic fallacy in the Middle Ages and unattainable today. A chorus of women in the room agreed.

In the middle of this invective on the state of men in our world, I broke into the room unannounced. I walked over to Pam's desk—which was inconveniently located in the middle of the room. I placed a dozen red roses on her desk, whispered "I love you," gave her a kiss, and left the room as quickly as I came in.

"Is it your birthday?" the startled professor asked Pam.

"No."

"Your anniversary?"

"No."

"Then what's the reason?"

"I guess he just wanted me to know he loves me and believes in me."

I fought Pam in a big way as she tried to pursue her dream. I wanted her to know in just as big a way that I believed in her dream.

"Iron sharpens iron, and one man sharpens another" (Prov. 27:17).

Waffle, how can you sharpen your wife so her dreams can

become reality? _____

_____

Spaghetti, what would you like your husband to do to help you

pursue your dreams? _____

_____

Share your response with your spouse. Commit your dreams to the Lord.

HOW A SPAGHETTI CAN ENCOURAGE HER WAFFLE

What can a woman do to help her husband be effective in his career pursuits? Keep it simple! When your husband feels he has the freedom to focus on work, he gains confidence about his ability to succeed. When your husband senses his work is part of the family's schedule rather than an interruption to it, his desire to help shape the kids' character will grow. When you say you are proud of him for the work he does, he leaves for work with renewed motivation. It sounds silly, but the key to helping your husband is to give him your permission to succeed.

When Pam and I moved to the San Diego area so I could begin my career as a senior pastor, I was very excited. I was convinced God had called me to preach and minister to families. I hit the pavement running. It required pretty intense focus on my part to learn the current processes of the church and diagnose the changes that needed to be made. I assumed Pam was right behind me, in step with the vision.

She was just as committed as I was to the success of our new pursuit, but she was facing different pressures. She was the primary caretaker of our two preschool boys, and we were living in a two-bedroom apartment. Children were not allowed to play on the sidewalk, on the grass, or in the common areas of the apartment complex. The only place kids were allowed to play was on the playground—on the other side of the complex.

Pam is usually a very positive individual, but the stress of dealing with two toddlers in a "no playing zone" was more than she could handle. Instead of being proud of me I heard things like, "Why did you do this to me?" "How long do we have to live like this?" "Are you ever going to do anything to get us out of this hole?" Coming home after a long day of work was like volunteering for an interrogation.

I knew I needed to go home and invest in my family, but I wanted to spend more time at work. Things were working there and everybody seemed to appreciate my efforts. Pam didn't like the fact that it was easier for me to be at work than with her, but she agreed it was a critical time in our life.

I (Pam) had given up a nice house, great friends, and a satisfying leadership role for sanctified insanity! Over the next few weeks, depression hit me like a tidal wave. I was struggling with who I was, what my new role would be in this church and community, and how I would survive such a drastic change.

One day I went to the closet to get a box off the top shelf. In reaching for the box, everything fell on me and scattered across the floor. "I hate it here!" I cried. The next thing I knew, I was sitting on top of a load of dirty laundry and sobbing! I don't know how long I sat there before my two little boys toddled in.

"Mommy, what's wrong?" they asked.

I gathered them onto my lap and rocked them as I prayed, "God, I know this is not the abundant life you planned! Bill has been paying a huge price. He's been coming home to my complaints and whining. I have been believing lies about him. I've said some awful things. Help me figure out what to do!"

I pulled out my Bible and read a very familiar passage in Ephesians 5. One phrase seemed to be in neon lights. It said the wife must respect her husband (see v. 22). I looked at it again. Are you sure, God? Isn't there a loophole for situations like mine? Over the next few days I read the dictionary and thesaurus looking up synonyms for honor and respect. I came up with three things I needed to do: 1) see Bill as God sees Bill—a man worthy of respect because God created him; 2) talk to Bill the way God talks to Bill—with loving, encouraging but honest words; 3) treat Bill like God treats Bill—by building him up with kindness.

A few days later I called Bill and asked if I could take him to lunch. He accepted rather tentatively. He wasn't sure what he was going to get.

Over lunch I reached across the table, took his hand, and said, "I'm sorry for the way I have treated you. If I never get the things I think will make me happy, that's okay. From this day forward I am on your team!"

I (Bill) can hardly explain the impact those words had on me. The most important opinion to me is Pam's. When she says I am doing well, I truly believe I am doing well regardless of what others say. When she is disappointed or critical, my heart sinks. I want to immediately change her opinion; and if I run into a roadblock, I instinctively want to shut her out of my career decisions. When she said, "I am on your team," my perspective on life was transformed. A few days after that lunch it became clear to me how to move my family into a rental home with a yard. I also began to see how to spend more strategic time with the family. All of this added together to simplify my relationship with her, which freed me to concentrate on my work more effectively. Pam made my life simpler with her commitment to be on my team and that made all the difference.

According to Romans 8:31, who is always on your side?

_____

Why does that make all the difference to you?

_____

Identify an issue that has left you and your spouse at odds.

_____

Will you commit to respect and love your spouse in this issue, even if you never get the things you think will make you happy?
☒ yes ☒ no ☒ I'm working on it, but I'm not there yet.

If you answered yes, let your spouse know you are on his or her side. If you did not answer yes, keep praying about it!

Deliberate Dreams

What can you do as a couple to make your pursuits more effective? Be deliberate. The differences in the sexes will lead to some predictable outcomes if you do not deliberately set goals and organize responsibilities. If left unchecked, the husband becomes more and more focused on his career and spends increasing numbers of hours in the pursuit of financial success. Meanwhile, more and more of the responsibilities of the home become hers to manage. The end result is that she feels taken advantage of and he feels unappreciated. Nobody grows closer to people who take advantage of them and make them feel unappreciated. A couple without goals will either live a very simple existence so this cycle never starts, or they will see the slow and steady deterioration of their love. Couples with goals they agree on will find their achievements make them more interesting people who consistently have new material to talk about.

In some marriages one spouse likes and desires goals while the other drags his or her feet. That can be manageable with a good attitude. Bill likes the concept of goal-setting, but early on I discovered he didn't like the process of writing out goals. So I interviewed him. Each year, usually as we travel on family vacation, Bill and I talk about our plans and review where we are and where we're going. I record the conversation in the form of written goals. Then, because I'm not fond of spreadsheets, Bill writes financial objectives that need to be accomplished to fund our dreams. After this process, we sit down and reevaluate our goals, make scheduling adjustments, discard some, and place some in a "not now, but in the future" file. We try to use each of our strengths to benefit our team.

Often in the areas of achievement, goal-setting, and dream-building couples struggle with how much to trust God and how much to be proactive and work hard. Read Psalm 37:3-9 and 2 Thessalonians 3:7-13. On the chart below, list your part and God's part in achieving your goals.

My Part	God's Part

Get to the Heart of the Matter

THE HEART OF A WOMAN: SECURITY

Security is your wife's most pervasive need. She longs to know that life with you is safe. She wants to be assured of physical safety, financial safety, social safety, and emotional safety. To build confidence that she is safe, she continually asks a series of questions to confirm her security is intact.

The strategy for answering her questions is simple in concept and complicated in practice. Look for the security need first and the related issues become manageable. If you keep this in mind, you will find that most issues can be discussed with your wife in a sane and logical fashion.

Question 1: Am I more important than our money? She knows money is important and she wants your family to be successful, but inside her heart she needs to know you are not so consumed with making and managing money that you lose sight of who she is. As long as she knows you consider her more valuable than your cash flow, she will be reasonable and cooperative in your financial decisions. If she feels she needs to compete with money for your attention, she will make sure money takes second place.

When emotional needs come to the surface, they demand expression and often complicate our lives. The key is to acknowledge them with compassion. When the emotional needs of our lives are acknowledged and compassionately accepted, they find their fulfillment and soften.

When a man deliberately spends money on his wife to communicate to her that she is valuable to him, he reaches straight to her heart. When a wife feels she is a financial priority to her husband, her heart moves closer to him.

Read Matthew 6:24-25 in your Bible. What prevailing attitude toward money do both husband and wife need to have?

_____

Waffle, what does this truth mean for you specifically?

_____

Spaghetti, what does this truth mean for you specifically?

_____

Question 2: Are you being sincere? "Pam, you are beautiful. I knew it when I married you, and I am even more convinced now that there is no one on earth as attractive as you." I thought I was being pretty smooth with those words. Pam was feeling self-conscious about herself during the year after the birth of our third son. I was very much in love with her, and I wanted her to know I still thought she was a pretty woman. Her response was, "You are just saying that because you have to. You don't really mean it."

It drives me crazy when she does this! Even if I am not being sincere, I want my words to soften her heart and draw her to me. She, on the other hand, goes through a very different process. Because everything in her life is connected to everything else, trust is a never-ending pursuit. When Pam trusts me, she trusts me with everything. When she opens her heart in one area, all the other areas of her life feel the need to open up also. If she is confident that I am sincere in my devotion and compliments, she feels it is safe to trust me. If she thinks I am just flattering her with my words, she will be reluctant to trust me emotionally because she feels she is setting herself up to be hurt.

Question 3: Do you notice me? Every wife wants to know her husband thinks about her, likes to be with her, and notices the newness in her life. This is one of the reasons conversation is important to your wife. She wants to know if you think her words are important and attractive. She wants to know you are interested in the way she thinks and you want to share with her the way you think. A wise husband schedules regular time just to visit with his wife.

The other obvious way this question manifests itself is in the way your wife fishes for compliments. We even see great people in the Bible fishing for compliments. In Song of Songs 2:1-2, King Solomon's bride, the Shulamite, prods him with the following words, "I am a rose of Sharon, a lily of the valleys."

The rose of Sharon and the lily of the valley were the most common flowers growing on the hills around her parents' farm. She is saying, "I am just a plain country girl. There is nothing special about me. How could you as a king choose someone like me who lacks any real beauty?" To say the least, she is feeling insecure. If Solomon agrees with her, he might as well make reservations for the doghouse!

His response is remarkable. "Like a lily among thorns, so is my darling among the young women" (v. 2). How did he come up with that one on the spur of the moment? We know her heart melted because of her response. "Like an apricot tree among the trees of the forest, so is my love among the young men" (v. 3). When is the last time you saw an apricot tree in the forest? She is letting him know there has never been a man like him, because he hit the target of her heart dead center.

Question 4: Am I more important than your sleep? It was the last day of our honeymoon, and we were experiencing what I (Bill) believed to be the best of all possible worlds. We were in Lake Tahoe enjoying the newness of our marriage. We needed to get up very early the next morning to catch our flight to Idaho, so I figured we should go to bed early. This seemed very reasonable to me, but I forgot to ask Pam what she had in mind.

During the next three hours, I heard about every boyfriend she ever had. She told me she wanted to share every detail of her life with me. As a young, idealistic husband I concurred and thought it would actually be possible to listen to Pam with the same level of attention with which she was sharing herself.

I held my own for the first hour. I became a little restless during the second hour. The third hour was a disaster. In the middle of a sentence I started to doze off, but I caught myself without her realizing I was losing it. Some time after that I fell fast asleep while she was baring her soul. I was awakened to a "heartquake" that registered 3.5 on our bed.

Pam was convulsively sobbing, murmuring, "I thought you loved me. How could you fall asleep on me? Am I really that boring?"

I sat up in bed, looked her in the eyes, and said, "I really do love you. I am so sorry for falling asleep. Go ahead and finish. I will listen to you talk about the men who came before me but couldn't capture your heart."

Pam pushed the issue, "You don't really want to hear it. You are just saying you will listen because you have to."

With a little bit of desperation in my voice, I reassured her, "No, I really want to know. Every detail of your life is important to me."

"Do you really mean it?"

"Yes, Pam. I really mean it!"

"Okay," she said with a glint in her eye, "I want to tell you about the country western songs I listened to growing up." Then she started singing!

I had been had. Here I was trying to address Pam's stated concern, and I totally missed the real issue. The concern on her heart was, "Bill, am I more important to you than your sleep? Are you willing to be tired to show me that I have first place in your heart?"

Question 5: Do you notice other women? This is one of the hardest to recognize and respond to strategically. Your wife will ask you, "What do you think of that woman's haircut?"

At times the right answer is "What woman?" One time your wife will be touched by your dedicated affection and feel closer to you for protecting her unique value in your life. The next time she will criticize you for being blind to her cosmetic priorities and will give you the cold shoulder.

At other times the right answer is, "Yes, I did. I think her haircut is cute. I even think you might look good in a style like that." One time she will be impressed that you would think about what would look good on her. The next time she will be offended you even noticed the other woman had hair.

This question applies to noticing body types, clothing styles, modesty, and attitudes. We are required to be aware of the ploys and practices of women without really noticing there are other women in the world. We need to treat all women with respect but only treat our wives with interest. We are supposed to notice that our wife is the most beautiful of all women without ever comparing her to another woman.

Waffle, read Job 31:1. How can you handle your visual bent in a godly

manner? _____

Spaghetti, read 1 Peter 3:3-4. How can you find lasting security in

your appearance? _____

BE HER MIRROR

We discovered the power of encouraging words while on our honeymoon. I (Pam) had just stepped from the shower and was looking in the mirror. I began to criticize my body. I went on for a few minutes until Bill could stand it no longer. He was angry that I would put down his choice of a wife. I was not only tearing myself down but undermining Bill's taste. Instead of saying something in anger he prayed, "God, I can do a better job than that mirror!"

He stood up, wrapped his arms around me, and told me to look straight into his eyes. He seriously and lovingly said, "I will be your mirror. My eyes will reflect your beauty. You are beautiful, Pamela. You are perfect. If you ever doubt it, come stand before me. The mirror of my eyes will tell you the true story. You are perfect for me. If I have to throw away every mirror in the house to get you to believe me, I will! From now on, let me be your mirror!"

THE HEART OF MAN: SIMPLICITY

Bill and I were asked to speak to a group of college students on our book Single Men Are Like Waffles–Single Women Are Like Spaghetti, and I (Pam) made the statement, "Ladies, what men want is a low-maintenance woman who will make the stress level of his life go down!" The males in the audience gave me a standing ovation! Your husband wants to know that life will be simpler and easier with you in it!

Because men compartmentalize life and have a problem-solving bent, they are drawn to the boxes where they think they can succeed. As a result of this pursuit of success, men like to keep life as simple as possible. The simpler life is, the fewer boxes they have to deal with. When things get complicated, they become demotivated and begin to detach from some boxes so they can simplify life. A wise wife helps her husband take a simple approach to life.

Men ask several questions to keep their lives simple enough to succeed:

Question 1: Is life with you going to be filled with admiration? Because men love to succeed, they drink up compliments the way babies devour milk. The cousin to compliments is flirting. When a woman flirts with a man, the box he happens to be in at the moment ignites with enthusiasm. Compliments from the woman he loves fill his soul with confidence.

After more than two decades of being married to the same woman, I am still amazed at how her compliments energize me and, conversely, how her negative assessments of my life set me back. A wife's compliments give her husband confidence, her flirting makes him feel sexy, her suggestions motivate him to change.

A word spoken at the right time is like golden apples
on a silver tray. A wise correction to a receptive ear
is like a gold ring or an ornament of gold.
Proverbs 25:11-12

Spaghetti, what "golden apple" can you give your husband

today? _____

Waffle, what box do you need admiration in right now?

_____

What perfect word or wise correction would be just what you

need to hear? _____

Question 2: Is life with you going to be free from complications? Men love to be thought of as heroes, and they love to do the things they are good at. As a result, they sometimes become overwhelmed when life gets too complicated. This can cause tension for a married couple. While the man is focused on the areas he can succeed in, his wife is processing their entire life. She sees her needs, the kids' needs, the financial needs, the vacation plans, and her hope for their next date all at the same time. While he is trying to simplify matters, she feels he is neglecting important areas of their life. A wife is most understanding when she considers ways she and her husband can work together to uncomplicate life.

Question 3: Is life with you going to be sexual? Men don't set out to be unreasonable about sex with their wives, but they often find themselves sexually restless when they are together. She walks by and he notices the way her hips move. She smiles at him and he instantly feels sexy. He walks into the bedroom while she is changing her clothes, and he immediately thinks this might be a great opportunity. Men know this kind of thinking is unreasonable and even accept that they shouldn't be this way, but none of them are very good at changing it. They tell themselves this is crazy, but nothing they try removes the tension except sex. As a result, men are embarrassingly in need of their wives' sexual attention.

Question 4: Is life with you going to be cooperative? When men bring up a topic for conversation, they intend to talk about that topic. So when a husband tells his wife they need to talk about the budget, he wants to talk about the budget. If they talk through their money issues and a decision is made, the husband immediately assumes this decision is solid. If his wife, however, was merely exploring her emotions about the budget rather than deciding on the budget, she may find herself not sticking to the conclusions of their discussion.

Question 5: Is life with you going to be lived in the present? Because men like to live in one box at a time, they tend to focus on the present. They don't remember details of their past as readily as women because they don't create as many emotional attachments to the events of their past. Men want to preserve the dignity of the present.

When Pam and I were newlyweds, I was able to give her my undivided attention. She was fun to be with and our life was very undemanding. I lavished her with words, simple gifts, and lots of time. For the first four years of our life together, it was easy to keep this up. Then we started having kids.

With each child, our schedule became more complicated and our financial needs grew. As a result, my commitment to my career grew. At the same time, my opportunity to lavish her with attention was diminishing. More work hours meant less time with her. My children's needs were stealing time and energy away from Pam. If she had continued to expect the same romantic overtures from me that I was able to give early on, I would have become very frustrated. Pam broadened her acceptance of my contribution to her life to include the big picture of what I was doing, and I have continued to fall even deeper in love with her.

Men long for success in the same way women long for security. Men want to do everything they can succeed in and very little they fall short in. They are attracted to everything their wives do that makes them feel successful. Women want to feel safe in all areas of their lives and are attracted to everything their husbands do to make them feel secure.

When things get tense in your relationship, see if the underlying issue is one of security or simplicity.

Think of the last time things got tense in your marriage. Briefly describe that time.

_____

Was this tension due to
☒ the husband's need for simplicity?
☒ the wife's need for security?

How would you handle the matter differently now?

_____

THE HEART OF GOD: YOU!

When people sense there's something special in a recipe, they probe a little and ask, "What's in this?" For over 27 years people have asked us how we stay in love and how our love stays fresh and strong. People ask us for the secret ingredient.

That special something in our relationship is the grace and strength we each receive from our relationship with God. This ingredient really isn't too secret because He wants us to know Him and the plan He has for our lives as husband and wife. (If you would like to know more about how to receive this grace in your own life, see page 113.) The source and strength to love another springs from the love God gives us.

Read Ecclesiastes 4:9-12 in your Bible. Complete the equation below to find the secret ingredient to every happy marriage.

_____
(your name)

+ _____
(your spouse's name)

+ _____

= A strong, happy marriage!

SPAGHETTI "Submitting to one another in the fear of Christ" (Eph. 5:21).

Why is voluntary, mutual submission necessary for unity, achievement, and fulfillment in the home?

_____

_____

Read Ephesians 5:22-24 in your Bible.

Using a separate sheet of paper, identify ways you will show respect to your husband by:
1. seeing him as God sees him.
2. talking to him the way God talks to him.
3. treating him the way God treats him.
4. letting him know he's your hero.
5. keeping his life simple.

Share your responses with your husband. Are you on the right track? If not, listen as he tells you what he really needs from you.

The three strands of you, your spouse, and God are an unbreakable team. As long as you keep God in the equation and seek to know Him and obey Him, your marriage will be fun and fulfilling. After all, it was God who created marriage!

1. L. C. Embrey and J. J. Fox, "Gender Differences in the Investment Decision-Making Process," Financial Counseling and Planning, 8, no. 2 (1997), 33-40, quoted in Bill and Pam Farrel, Men Are Like Waffles—Women Are Like Spaghetti (Eugene, OR: Harvest House, 2001), 128.
2. Ibid.
3. Susan Roxburgh, "Exploring the Work and Family Relationship," Journal of Family Issues 20, no. 6 (1999): 771-88, quoted in Bill and Pam Farrel, Men are Like Waffles—Women are Like Spaghetti, 128.
4. Kaia Rendahl, Jean Anderson, Kristin Hill, Anna Henning, Christopher Randall, Amy Davis, Psychology Group at St. Olaf University, results of survey.
5. Ahalya Krishnan and Christopher J. Sweeney, "Gender Differences in Fear of Success Imagery and Other Achievement-Related Background Variables Among Medical Students," Sex Roles: A Journal of Research, August, 1998, http://www.findarticles.com (accessed January 18, 2007).
6. Ibid.
7. Maria Gardiner and Marika Tiggemann, "Gender Differences in Leadership Style, Job Stress and Mental Health in Male- and Female-Dominated Industries," Journal of Occupational and Organizational Psychology 72, no. 3 (September 1999), 301.

WAFFLE

"Submitting to one another in the fear of Christ" (Eph. 5:21).

Why is voluntary, mutual submission necessary for unity, achievement, and fulfillment in the home?

_____

_____

Read Ephesians 5:25-28 in your Bible.

Using a separate sheet of paper, identify ways you will love your wife sacrificially by:
1. loving her as Christ loved the church.
2. encouraging her to become all God intends for her to be.
3. loving her as you love your own body.
4. being her mirror.
5. letting her know she's secure with you.

Share your responses with your wife. Are you on the right track?
If not, listen as she tells you what she really needs from you.

I Will Be Your Mirror

Words and Music by Boomer & Lisa Reiff (www.lisareiff.com)

She looked into the mirror on that sacred night
Hoping her reflection had somehow changed
The image looking back at her wasn't what she wanted to see

Mirror, mirror on the wall …

As he watched her from a distance he could read her mind
He knew the way she felt and how her heart cried out
And he wondered at this lovely girl—how she could be so blind
'Cause when he looked at her the only thing he saw was beautiful …

I will be your mirror
Reflecting the beauty of your face
You are lovely and gentle
A picture of God's amazing grace
I will see in you what you can't see in yourself
And I will tell you again and again
I will be your mirror

She turned back from the mirror and felt her heart sink low
As she told him all the things she'd like to change
Her smile, her eyes, her nose, her skin—she would change them if she could
How many times she'd prayed that she could just feel beautiful …
So he took her face into his hands as he spoke the words so true
Look to me for your reflection and I promise you, I promise you …

I will be your mirror
Reflecting the beauty of your face
You are lovely and gentle
A picture of God's amazing grace
I will see in you what you can't see in yourself
And I will tell you again and again
I will be your mirror

And now she looks back on her life—at all the years that have come and gone
And she knows the gift he gave that day became the ground she's walked upon
When he said …

I will be your mirror
Reflecting the beauty of your face
You are lovely and gentle
A picture of God's amazing grace
I will see in you what you can't see in yourself
And I will tell you again and again
I will be your mirror.

Tap Into God's Strength

Throughout this study we talk about the grace and strength we receive from our relationship with God. God wants you to know Him and the plan He has for your life. But how can you tap into God's strength? How can you receive His grace for your own life and for the marriage you desire to have?

One of the greatest desires we have on this earth is loving and being loved by someone else. God wants us to love Him above anyone or anything else because loving Him puts everything else in life in perspective. In God we find the hope, peace, and joy that are possible only through a personal relationship with Him. Through His presence in our lives, we can truly love our spouses, because God is love. The source and strength of love springs from the love God first gave us. "We love because He first loved us" (1 John 4:19).

John 3:16 says, "God loved the world in this way: He gave His One and Only Son, so that everyone who believes in Him will not perish but have eternal life." In order to live our earthly lives "to the full" (see John 10:10, NIV), we much accept God's gift of love.

A relationship with God begins by admitting that we are not perfect and continue to fall short of God's standards. Romans 3:23 says, "All have sinned and fall short of the glory of God." The price for these wrongdoings is separation from God. "The wages [or price] of sin is death, but the gift of God is eternal life in Christ Jesus our Lord" (Rom. 6:23).

God's love comes to us right in the middle of our sin. "God proves His own love for us in that while we were still sinners Christ died for us!" (Rom. 5:8). He doesn't ask us to clean up our lives first—in fact, without His help we are incapable of living by His standards.

Forgiveness begins when we admit our sin to God. When we do, He is faithful to forgive and restore our relationship with Him. "If we confess our sins, He is faithful and righteous to forgive us our sins and to cleanse us from all unrighteousness" (1 John 1:9).

This love gift and relationship with God is not just for a special few but for everyone. "Everyone who calls on the name of the Lord will be saved" (Rom. 10:13). If you would like to receive God's gift of salvation, pray this prayer:

> Jesus, I am sorry I have chosen to live apart from You. I want You in my life.
> I accept the payment of love You gave for me by Your death on the cross.
> Thank You for being my best friend and my God.

If you prayed this prayer for the first time, let us be the first to welcome you to God's family! Share your experience with your small-group leader, your pastor, or a trusted Christian friend. To grow in your new life in Christ, continue to cultivate this new relationship through Bible study, prayer, and fellowship with other Christians.

Key Thoughts for Small-Group Leaders[1]

THE INFLUENCE OF SMALL GROUPS

Small groups are one of the most effective ways to promote growth in people's lives. The relationships that form in the small-group experience naturally result in encouragement, accountability, and motivation. The members of the group support one another through prayer, listening to one another's stories, and sharing the growth that is taking place in their lives.

Small groups are based on the power of friendship. We all become like the people we hang around. Over time, small-group members are influenced by how others in the group think, talk, and make decisions. An organized small group takes this power and focuses it so the influence happens faster. This commitment to pass on truth through relationships keeps the path of growth personal, practical, and powerful.

ORGANIZING YOUR SMALL GROUP

A simple way to organize your small group is to balance your group's activities around the five great loves of the Bible:
• Love for God (Matt. 22:37)—Have someone in the group lead a time of prayer each week.
• Love for God's Word (2 Tim. 3:16-17)—Lead the group in a Bible discussion each week.
• Love for God's People (John 13:35)—Ensure the place you meet is clean, comfortable, and inviting.
• Love for Pre-Believers (2 Cor. 5:17-21)—Encourage everyone in your group to pray for five friends who do not know Jesus.

• Love for Ministry (Eph. 4:11-13)—Pray that God raises up a leader in your group to begin another group when your study is completed.

1. Adapted from Bill Farrel, Small Group Training 2004. For more information about small-group training visit www.farrelcommunications.com.

Leader Guide

OVERVIEW AND STUDY FORMAT

This leader guide provides directions for leading a seven-session, small-group study. A leader kit is also available (1415832161), containing DVDs with Bill and Pam Farrel's video messages to be used during the group sessions.

Because these video messages are valuable to the study, we recommend you purchase a leader kit to be used in your small group. However, the study can be done without the video messages. If you do not use the DVDs, you may choose not to have an introductory session. If so, make certain participants have their books in time to complete week 1 before your first session.

Each session in this leader guide is divided into five main segments with suggestions for leading the session. You may revise these ideas to fit the personality of your group, the needs of the group, and your time schedule. The video segments vary in length from session to session. As you plan your meeting each week, use this as an opportunity to be creative with your small-group sessions and provide variety for your group members.

Let's take a look at what makes up the five segments in each small-group session.

1. Appetizers is a time for welcome, announcements, and an icebreaker activity to help participants become comfortable with one another.

2. Family Meal provides questions to guide the group to discuss what they learned in their

personal Bible study the past week.

3. Waffles and Spaghetti provides time for husbands and wives to privately compare their responses to the activities in their personal weekly study.

4. TV Dinner allows participants to view Bill and Pam Farrel on video as they introduce the material for the following week of individual study. Each video session will introduce participants to the material they will study the next week. There is no video to view in session 7 when you discuss the week 6 material. It is highly recommended that you go ahead and have that final session to discuss week 6, share personal highlights from your study, and celebrate your marriages!

5. Divine Dessert gives suggestions for leading participants in a time of prayer.

If you are using the DVDs, you will find a promotional segment (disc 2) for you to use to raise awareness of the study. You will also find the "I Will Be Your Mirror" music video (disc 2). This video is included in session 6 but has been placed on the DVD separately for easy use at any point in the study.

As you prepare to lead a small group through Men Are Like Waffles–Women Are Like Spaghetti, take a few minutes to view "A Word to Leaders" on disc 2. There the Farrels share their hearts about the effectiveness of small groups and pray for you as a leader.

Being a Small-Group Leader

You don't need to be a gifted teacher, natural leader, or the perfect spouse to facilitate these small-group sessions. What do you need to be?

Be spiritual. If you hunger to connect with your Heavenly Father and your spouse in a deeper way, and you have a desire to help couples love one another and God more intimately, then you are just the person (or couple) to lead this study.

Be personal. Greet each couple as they arrive. Don't skip the Appetizer (icebreaking) segment of the small-group time. Participants need this time to get comfortable with one another and with the idea of discussing God's plan for marriage with others.

Be early. Have the room set up for easy conversation with chairs in a circle and the TV in a place it can be easily viewed by everyone. Simple refreshments would be nice, as would some candlelight and romantic music. (Maybe not the first time—it might scare off the men!)

Be considerate. Provide childcare. Ask the Lord to meet this need and He will! Since childcare is an issue, begin and end each session on time. As hard as it may be to start the sessions on time—do so! Invite couples to stay for further discussion or fellowship afterward if they desire, but provide a clear end so parents can leave to get their kids without feeling bad. Let them know you are available for questions, encouragement, and prayer.

Leading a Small Group

Ask God to put together the small group He desires for this study. A group of six couples is ideal for free sharing of thoughts and ideas. If you have more than that, consider breaking into smaller groups.

Announce the study in your church newsletter, bulletin, and on bulletin boards. Encourage couples to invite unchurched friends to participate. Use the promotional segment on the DVD before or after worship services to introduce couples to the study.

In preparation for each small-group session, complete the assignments in the member book. The most effective way you can guide this study is by allowing God's Word to transform you and your marriage, and then letting that transformation overflow to the men and women in your small group. Read through the leader guide suggestions for each session. Adapt them to meet the needs of your group and the length of your sessions.

After each session, evaluate the group experience. Are you asking effective questions? Did one person tend to monopolize the discussions while others didn't speak at all? Do some activities tend to make emotions run high or couples pick at each other? Did you have time to pray? Commit the study to God and ask Him to give you wisdom as you lead this group.

SESSION 1

BEFORE THE SESSION

1. Have copies of Men Are Like Waffles–Women Are Like Spaghetti ready for distribution. Husbands and wives need their own personal copy of the member book. (Call your local LifeWay Christian Store a few weeks ahead of time to make sure they have enough in stock. If not, they will be happy to order copies for you.)

2. Prepare a sign-in sheet for participants to write their names, addresses, phone numbers, and e-mail addresses. Place this on a table near the door along with pens, markers, name tags, and a basket for collecting money if participants are paying for their member books. (A little basket with chocolates or mints would be nice as well!)

3. Read About the Authors and About the Study on pages 4-5. Be prepared to share your condensed version of this information.

4. Have the DVD cued for the session 1 video. This video is 40:20 in length.

DURING THE SESSION

Appetizer (Welcome and Opening)

1. As couples arrive, ask them to sign in, prepare name tags, and pick up copies of Men Are Like Waffles–Women Are Like Spaghetti. Invite them to leave payment for their books in the basket or offer to collect their money after the session.

2. Ask each couple to introduce themselves by telling their names, wedding anniversary date, and the story of how they met.

3. Invite participants to guess what they think is meant by men are like waffles and women are like spaghetti.

Family Meal (Group discussion)

1. Ask participants to leaf through week 1

(pp. 6-23) of the member book. Draw their attention to the weekly format of reading, learning activities, and waffle- and spaghetti-specific activities.

2. Use the suggestions in About the Study (p. 5) to explain how participants can get the greatest benefit from this study. Encourage husbands and wives to spend time together each week praying and discussing their answers. Let them know they will have couple time in your weekly sessions as well.

3. Explain the format of your small-group sessions— you will discuss the previous week's homework as a group and in couples, view the DVD where the Farrels introduce the material you will be studying over the next week, and conclude with prayer time.

4. Instruct participants to read and complete week 1 before next week's session.

Waffles and Spaghetti (Couple discussion)

1. Ask husbands and wives to talk together about what they hope to get out of this study personally and what they desire to happen in their marriage as a result of this study.

TV Dinner (View the video – 40:20)

1. Ask participants to turn to the viewer guide on page 7 of their member book. Invite them to take notes as they watch the DVD.

2. Begin the session 1 video—"Appreciating the Differences."

3. Pause the video just before the skit on the beach. Invite volunteers to identify what part of the Farrels' message they found most intriguing.

4. As you conclude your discussion, explain that the next portion of the presentation is about communication. Restart the DVD.

5. At the end of the video session the Farrels will pose a question to the couples: What are the benefits of a man being like a waffle and a woman being like spaghetti? They will have 4 minutes to discuss this question. You will not need to stop the DVD. A countdown is provided on the screen.

Divine Dessert (Prayer time)

Ask participants to stand in a circle with their hands touching the shoulders of the persons on either side of them. Instruct them to silently pray that God will place His hand of blessing on the persons they are touching.

Close with a prayer of blessing over the couples. You might pray something like this:

Father, Your Word says we love because You first loved us. Thank You for Your love. Help our love for one another grow through this study. Place Your hand of blessing on each couple so that our marriages will be an example of Your love for all the world to see.

SESSION 2

BEFORE THE SESSION

1. Cue the DVD to session 2. This video is 22:00 in length; plan your discussion time accordingly.
2. Take each couple's picture as they arrive. Develop two copies of each picture before next week; you will use them in session 3.

DURING THE SESSION

Appetizer
Which specific description of the differences between men and women in week 1 made you laugh hardest? Why? How were you particularly "noodly" or "waffly" this week?

Family Meal
1. What do you see as positive in the assertion that men view life in waffle boxes and women process life like spaghetti?
2. When is it hardest to accept the way the opposite gender is wired? What did you learn this week that makes accepting the differences easier? What Scriptures challenged you to accept and appreciate your spouse just the way he or she is?
3. What causes the most miscommunication in marriages? What did you learn this week that

will help you bridge that communication gap with your spouse?
4. The Farrels say understanding one another should not be our goal. What should be our goal? How did this week's study help you become a better listener?
5. Read aloud Proverbs 15:1; 16:24; and Ephesians 4:29. Give examples of gentle, pleasant, and uplifting words husbands and wives can speak to one another.

What would happen in marriages if these kinds of words were the priority in communication?

Waffles and Spaghetti
1. Share with your spouse what you recorded as true, noble, lovely, admirable, excellent and praiseworthy about him or her in the activity on page 18.
2. Discuss the waffle and spaghetti activity at the conclusion of week 1.
3. Encourage couples to spend time when they get home comparing their evaluation responses at the end of week 1 and brainstorming ways they can strengthen the weak areas (if they have not already done so).

TV Dinner (22:00)
1. Ask participants to turn to the viewer guide on page 25. Invite them to take notes as they watch the DVD.
2. Play the session 2 video—"Relaxing and De-stressing." If you want to split the video into two parts, pause at the end of the passwords section and give couples an opportunity to share possible passwords they might be able to use in their relationships. You will discuss this in more depth next week. Explain to the couples that the next portion of the video is about dealing with stress.
3. After viewing the rest of the video, invite volunteers to share what they found most meaningful, challenging, or encouraging from the video.

Divine Dessert

1. Ask each couple to hold hands. Direct the husbands to pray, thanking God for creating their wives in such a unique and valuable way and for how that difference benefits their marriage and family. Then ask the wives to pray, thanking God for creating their husbands to process life in boxes and for how that benefits their marriage and family.
2. Close in prayer for the entire group, basing your prayer on Romans 15:7.

SESSION 3

BEFORE THE SESSION

1. Cue up the DVD to session 3. This video is 16:16 in length.
2. Prepare and bring copies of the photos you took last week of each couple. (See Before the Session for session 2.)

DURING THE SESSION

Appetizer
Instruct couples to take turns giving each other a shoulder massage. Ask participants what stresses them out the most. Invite them to share which of the activities they are most likely to do when they get stressed: get a massage, go for a drive, shoot some basketball, journal, talk (add your own ideas).

Family Meal
1. What new insights did you gain about yourself and how you handle stress? What new insights did you gain into how your spouse processes stress?
2. How should the command in James 4:8 transform how both men and women process stress? What do we gain when we go to God with our stresses? How can you give personal testimony to this?

3. Share a time when your spouse deliberately chose to lower your stress level. What did he or she have to sacrifice to do so? How did you and your marriage benefit?
4. Read Proverbs 11:25. How did that verse motivate you? How have you sought to refresh your mate? How have you been refreshed in return?
5. Without naming the irritation, name the positive trait of your mate you selected to focus on when your spouse's idiosyncrasies start to bug you. How has focusing on the positive affected your attitude?
6. What is the point of passwords? If you were able to create a password, share it with your group. If you are still in the process, share a happy memory from your marriage and see if the group can help you brainstorm how to turn that positive experience into a password.
7. What did you discover or acknowledge about yourself in the area of resting?
8. How does God give you rest when there's no time to rest?

Waffles and Spaghetti
1. Compare your responses under "We Process Stress Differently" on pages 27-28. Discuss specific ways you can help one another process the stresses you know you'll face in the coming week.
2. Discuss the Waffle and Spaghetti activity at the conclusion of week 2 (pp. 38-39).

TV Dinner (16:16)
1. Request participants turn to the viewer guide on page 41. Invite them to take notes as they watch the DVD.
2. Play the session 3 video—"Living and Loving." Close to the end of the video presentation, the Farrels will instruct couples to "Whisper one thing to your spouse that doesn't cost money but expresses love to you." You can let the DVD run. Time is provided for couples to complete this activity.
3. Invite volunteers to share what they found the

most meaningful, challenging, or encouraging from the video.

Divine Dessert

1. Give each couple the two pictures you made of them. Ask them to write their names and a prayer request relating specifically to their marriage or family on the back of one of the photos. (The other photo is for them to keep.) Place all those pictures in a basket. Then ask each couple to draw one picture from that basket.

2. Direct couples to spend time praying for the need specified on the back of the photo they drew from the basket. Suggest they place the photo in a prominent place in their home as a reminder to pray daily for this couple throughout this study.

3. Close in prayer, asking God to give each couple the means and opportunity to get away soon to rest and renew their love.

SESSION 4

BEFORE THE SESSION

1. Cue the DVD to session 4. This video is 43:33 in length, so your Family Meal and Waffle and Spaghetti discussion times will need to be shorter. If you don't utilize the DVD in your group sessions, your discussion time can be its normal length, but handle this topic with discretion and sensitivity.

2. Place a poster board, chalkboard, tear sheets, or some other large writing surface in your meeting room for use during the Appetizer.

DURING THE SESSION

Appetizer

Ask couples to describe their favorite date spots in your area. Make two lists on a large writing surface: one list for the really nice expensive dating opportunities in your area and another list of romantic opportunities that cost $10 or less.

Family Meal

1. If you could go anywhere in the world on a romantic rendezvous with your spouse, where would you want to go and why?

2. What "looking back" date did you take this week?

3. Is a lack of funds a valid excuse for not having romance in your marriage? Why? Share an idea off your dream date list. How can that idea be adapted to fit within a limited budget?

4. Read Hebrews 3:13. How did learning about biblical encouragement change your view of romance? What did you learn that you can apply to your marriage?

5. How did studying God's view of sex give you a different perspective or greater appreciation of physical intimacy within marriage?

6. What are some boundaries couples can establish to protect their intimacy?

Waffles and Spaghetti

1. Discuss boundaries you need to set around your relationship.

2. Discuss the waffle and spaghetti activity at the conclusion of week 3 (pp. 58-59). End your couple time by praying together as suggested in that same activity.

TV Dinner (43:33)

1. Ask participants to turn to the viewer guide on page 61. Invite them to take notes as they watch the DVD.

2. Play the session 4 video—"Handling Conflict." Because this session includes the testimonies of both Pam and Bill, it's longer than the other sessions. If you need to take a break, a good time to do that would be just before the Farrels get into the Six Statements of Forgiveness.

3. After finishing the video, invite volunteers to share what they found most meaningful, challenging, or encouraging from the message. Acknowledge that this video session was rather intense. If your time is running short, let participants know you will allow time at next week's session to further discuss and process what they heard today. This session may

bring up some painful issues for individuals in your group. Don't get in over your head. Provide the support you can and be prepared to refer them to a counselor or staff member if necessary.

Divine Dessert
1. Invite someone to close your group in prayer. Remind participants to continue praying for their "prayer photo" couple.
2. Ask couples to bring a photograph from their wedding next week.

SESSION 5

BEFORE THE SESSION

1. Contact participants and remind them to bring a wedding photo to the session.
2. Cue the DVD to session 5. This video segment is only 8:55 in length, so you will have more time for discussion. Remember to allow extra time for any discussion you weren't able to wrap up last week.

DURING THE SESSION

Appetizer
Invite couples to pass around their wedding photos. Ask if anything went wrong at their wedding, or if they have been to weddings where things didn't go as planned. Remind them that there are no perfect weddings or marriages, which makes forgiveness vital to a successful marriage.
Family Meal
The video session last week (session 4) was fairly long and intense. You may want to take some time before you begin talking about the homework from week 4 to allow participants the opportunity to discuss what the Farrels shared last week.
1. What are the basic underlying causes for conflict in marriages? Is conflict always negative? What positive value can conflict have in a marriage?
2. How do the waffle and spaghetti differences between men and women influence how each

handles conflict? How did understanding that your spouse handles conflict differently than you help you not get quite so frustrated with him or her?
3. Read Colossians 3:12-13. What attitudes and actions are necessary if a husband and wife are going to fight for their relationship rather than with each other?
4. What did you learn about positive and negative ways to handle anger?
5. What rules do you have as a couple to make sure you "fight fair"? What ideas from this week might you add to your marital "rules of engagement"?
6. How did the biblical example of Joseph's forgiveness encourage and challenge you?
7. How can unforgiveness toward someone other than your spouse still adversely affect your relationship with your spouse?
8. What is the relationship between personal growth and a successful marriage?
9. Describe a time you blew it and someone extended forgiveness, grace, and mercy toward you. How was that a reflection of Christ? How did you feel? What do you need to sacrifice to extend that same forgiveness and grace to others?

Waffles and Spaghetti
1. Discuss the waffle and spaghetti activity at the end of week 4 (pp. 74-75).
2. Pray together, asking God to make you a forgiving family who spreads hope, joy, and love in the world.

TV Dinner (8:55)
1. Ask participants to turn to the viewer guide on page 77. Invite them to take notes as they watch the DVD.
2. Play the session 5 video—"Functioning as a Family."
3. Invite volunteers to share what they found most meaningful, challenging, or encouraging from the video.

Divine Dessert
1. Remind couples to continue praying for one another using the prayer photos they took home

after session 3.

2. Ask for prayer requests of specific family needs within your group. Allow time for personal prayer, then ask for a volunteer to pray for the specific needs mentioned.

SESSION 6

BEFORE THE SESSION

1. Cue the DVD to session 6. This final video segment is only 7:20 in length, so you will have more time for discussion.

DURING THE SESSION

Appetizer
Complete these statements: "The thing I most hate to do around the house is …" "The thing my spouse most hates to do around the house is …"

Family Meal
1. How do you decide who does what around the house? Have you ever traded roles? What did you learn by trading places?
2. What do the Farrels believe is the best way to delegate household tasks? How can expressing gratitude ease a lot of tension that can build up around the "who does what" issue?
3. How can understanding the waffle tendencies of your husband or noodle tendencies of your wife help you better understand how they take on tasks or expect tasks to be completed?
4. When you did the "what's important to me" exercise on pages 80-81, what was an area of tension where your spouse was a 3 and you were a 1? How did you resolve that tense issue?
5. Read Galatians 5:13. What key actions and attitudes should be evident in our marriages? How might true obedience to that verse change how you approach household tasks?
6. What biblical phrase did you choose to repeat

to yourself when you feel anger or resentment building? Did you try it this week? How did it work?
7. How do you think being a waffle or spaghetti influences the way you parent? Give an example of how you each react differently to the same situation with a child.
8. What insights did you gain into yourself or family members by analyzing personality types? How can understanding personality types help you be a better spouse and parent?
9. What other hints for raising sons and daughters can you add to the Farrels' insights?
10. What is one of the greatest favors you can do for your children according to Hebrews 12:5-11? Why?
11. Dads, how do you let your kids know you feel rewarded to be their dad? Moms, how do you let your kids know you rejoice they were born?

Waffles and Spaghetti
1. Thank one another for the tasks each of you perform in your home.
2. Discuss the waffle and spaghetti activities at the end of week 5 (pp. 92-93).

TV Dinner (7:20)
1. Ask participants to turn to the viewer guide on page 95. This week they will find an activity on this page. Instruct them to read through the activity and give it serious thought as they watch the DVD.
2. Play the session 6 video—"Succeeding Together."
3. Invite volunteers to share what they found the most meaningful, challenging, or encouraging from the video.

Divine Dessert
1. Ask each couple to pair up with one other couple. Invite them to share prayer requests relating to their children (or extended family if they have no children). Encourage all four people in each small group to pray or to choose one person to lead in prayer.

2. Close in prayer for the whole group, thanking God for creating families and asking for His help to serve one another through love.

SESSION 7

BEFORE THE SESSION

This session will be different because there is no video. Why don't you consider making this final session a celebration? Begin your celebration session with a spaghetti dinner. Then follow the discussion suggestions listed below. Once you have discussed the material and prayed together, conclude with

a waffle cone ice cream dessert. Enlist every member of the small group to help plan this celebration. The more involved they are in the process, the more they will enjoy it.

DURING THE SESSION

Appetizer
Enjoy a spaghetti dinner!

Family Meal
1. What did the Farrels say is meant by "building a life"? How will the wise husband and wife pursue their goals and seek to build a life? What does this look like on a daily basis?
2. What new insight did you gain on the different ways men and women achieve? According to Ephesians 6:6-8, what do Christian men and women have in common when it comes to work?
3. What did you learn from Scripture about the balance between working hard and trusting God?
4. What's necessary for both husband and wife to achieve their God-given dreams?
5. What did you learn beats in the heart of a woman? of a man? What changes did you make in the way you interact with your mate as result?
6. Bill and Pam say you can make your God-given

differences work "for you and for your relationship and family." In what ways have you seen this to be true in your marriage? What have you learned that can help you build your marriage based on your unique gender and strengths?
7. What is one change or adjustment you have made personally as a result of this study? How has it improved your marriage? What other changes would you like to begin applying to your personal life and your relationship with your spouse?

8. What is the secret ingredient to every happy marriage? How has that secret ingredient affected your marriage? How can we make sure that secret ingredient doesn't remain a secret? In other words, how can we as married couples share the love of Christ with others? (Urge participants to make certain they have personally received Jesus Christ as their Savior; offer to meet with them privately to discuss this further.)

Waffles and Spaghetti
1. Compare responses to the "iron sharpens iron" activity on page 100.
2. Discuss the waffle and spaghetti activity at the conclusion of week 6 (pp. 110-111).
3. Hold hands, look into your spouse's eyes, and relate at least one beautiful thing you see in one another. Commit to be each other's "mirror" of encouragement.

Divine Dessert
Close in prayer, basing your prayer for the group on Romans 12:10. (Or you may want to repeat the blessing prayer from Divine Desserts in session 1.)

Final Dessert
Enjoy some ice cream in a waffle cone and a great time of fellowship!

Expanded and Updated!